GREAT
POEMS

First published in 2005 by Miles Kelly Publishing Ltd
Bardfield Centre, Great Bardfield, Essex, CM7 4SL

Copyright © Miles Kelly Publishing Ltd 2005

This edition published 2009

10 9 8 7 6 5 4 3 2 1

Editorial Director Belinda Gallagher

Art Director Jo Brewer

Cover Designer Jo Brewer

Picture Researchers Laura Faulder,
Jennifer Hunt, Liberty Newton

Image Manager Lorraine King

Proofreader Margaret Berrill

Production Manager Elizabeth Brunwin

Reprographics Anthony Cambray, Ian Paulyn

Editions Manager Bethan Ellish

ISBN 978-1-84810-144-9

Printed in China

British Library Cataloguing-in-Publication Data
A catalogue record for this book is available from the British Library

Made with paper from a sustainable forest

www.mileskelly.net
info@mileskelly.net

www.factsforprojects.com
The one-stop homework helper
— pictures, facts, videos, projects and more

GREAT
POEMS

Dedicated to the memory of
Kate Miles

CONTENTS

WAR AND HEROISM 157

ANIMALS 189

CHILDREN'S POEMS 231

*W*IT AND HUMOUR 271

*I*NTO THE SHADOWS 305

WEATHER AND SEASONS 419

$\mathcal{L}$OVE

$\mathcal{L}$ove poems have produced some wonderfully familiar lines: 'How do I love thee? Let me count the ways'; 'Come live with me and be my love'; 'She walks in beauty like the night'; 'My love is like a red, red rose'; 'Shall I compare thee to a summer's day'; and 'Drink to me only with thine eyes'. In this section, the poets reveal their helter-skelter range of emotions in words that capture the ecstasy, joy and anguish of lovers over the centuries.

from The Bible

If I speak in the tongues of men and of angels, but
have not love, I am a noisy gong or a clanging cymbal.
And if I have prophetic powers, and understand all
mysteries and all knowledge, and if I have all faith, so
as to remove mountains, but have not love, I am
nothing. If I give away all I have, and if I deliver my
body to be burned, but have not love, I gain nothing.

Love is patient and kind; love is not jealous or
boastful; it is not arrogant or rude. Love does not
insist on its own way; it is not irritable or resentful;
it does not rejoice at wrong, but rejoices in the right.
Love bears all things, believes all things, hopes all
things, endures all things.

Love never ends; as for prophecies, they will pass
away; as for tongues, they will cease; as for
knowledge, it will pass away. For our knowledge is

imperfect and our prophecy is imperfect; but when the perfect comes, the imperfect will pass away. When I was a child, I spoke like a child, I thought like a child, I reasoned like a child; when I became a man, I gave up childish ways. For now we see in a mirror dimly, but then face to face. Now I know in part; then I shall understand fully, even as I have been fully understood. So faith, hope, love abide, these three; but the greatest of these is love.

St Paul

circa 50AD

I Corinthians 13: 1–13

*A*fter the death of Jesus, his apostles travelled around Asia Minor and the Mediterranean, establishing communities of disciples. Letters were a vital way of keeping in touch with these early churches, which needed constant teaching and support. More Bible letters are attributed to Paul than to any other apostle, and these inspiring lines, now often read aloud at weddings and on other significant occasions, are from Paul's first letter to the Corinthians.

Sonnets from the Portugese 43

How do I love thee? Let me count the ways.

I love thee to the depth and breadth and height

My soul can reach, when feeling out of sight

For the ends of Being and ideal Grace.

I love thee to the level of everyday's

Most quiet need, by sun and candlelight.

I love thee freely, as men strive for Right;

I love thee purely, as they turn from Praise.

I love thee with the passion put to use

In my old griefs, and with my childhood's faith.

I love thee with a love I seemed to lose

With my lost saints, – I love thee with the breath,

Smiles, tears, of all my life! – and, if God choose,

I shall but love thee better after death.

Elizabeth Barrett Browning
1806–61, b. England

*E*lizabeth Barrett picked up what education she could from her brother's tutor and became an accomplished scholar. She spent much of her life as an invalid, writing poetry for amusement. Poems (1844) was so successful that many suggested she should follow Wordsworth as Poet Laureate. Forbidden by her father to marry, in 1845 Elizabeth secretly corresponded with Robert Browning and eloped with him to Italy in 1846, where she lived happily until her death 15 years later.

The Passionate Shepherd to His Love

Come live with me and be my love,

And we will all the pleasures prove,

That hills and valleys, dales and fields,

And all the craggy mountains yields.

There we will sit upon the rocks,

And see the shepherds feed their flocks,

By shallow rivers to whose falls

Melodious birds sing madrigals.

And I will make thee beds of roses

With a thousand fragrant posies,

A cap of flowers, and a kirtle

Embroidered all with leaves of myrtle;

A gown made of the finest wool

Which from our pretty lambs we pull;

Fair linèd slippers for the cold,

With buckles of the purest gold;

A belt of straw and ivy buds,

With coral clasps and amber studs:

And if these pleasures may thee move,

Come live with me and be my love.

The shepherds' swains shall dance and sing

For thy delight each May morning:

If these delights thy mind may move,

Then live with me and be my love.

Christopher Marlowe
1564–93, b. England

P*laywright Christopher Marlowe was greatly admired by his contemporaries – Shakespeare and Ben Jonson, among others. Often in trouble with the law, he was killed in a pub brawl while quarrelling over the bill.*

This poem was published after his death in **The Passionate Pilgrim** *(1599) – a volume of poems attributed on the title page to Shakespeare, but in fact by various authors.*

She Walks in Beauty

She walks in beauty, like the night
Of cloudless climes and starry skies;
And all that's best of dark and bright
Meet in her aspect and her eyes:
Thus mellow'd to that tender light
Which heaven to gaudy day denies.

One shade the more, one ray the less,
Had half impair'd the nameless grace
Which waves in every raven tress,
Or softly lightens o'er her face;
Where thoughts serenely sweet express
How pure, how dear their dwelling-place.

And on that cheek, and o'er that brow,

So soft, so calm, yet eloquent,

The smiles that win, the tints that glow,

But tell of days in goodness spent,

A mind at peace with all below,

A heart whose love is innocent!

Lord Byron
1788–1824, b. England

Byron's poetry was frequently attacked by critics as immoral, yet was immensely popular. He was a controversial figure and found himself on the outside of English society.

He settled in Italy where he engaged in revolutionary activity. After financing, training and leading the Greeks in rebellion against the Turks, Byron died at only 36 years old.

A Red, Red Rose

My love is like a red, red rose
    That's newly sprung in June:
My love is like the melody
    That's sweetly played in tune.

As fair art thou, my bonnie lass,
    So deep in love am I:
And I will love thee still, my dear,
    Till a' the seas gang dry.

Till a' the seas gang dry, my dear,

   And the rocks melt wi' the sun:

And I will love thee still, my dear,

   While the sands o' life shall run.

And fare thee weel, my only love,

   And fare thee weel a while!

And I will come again, my love,

   Thou' it were ten thousand mile.

Robert Burns

1759–96, b. Scotland

Burns' Poems, Chiefly in the Scottish Dialect *(1786) made him an overnight success, acclaimed by Edinburgh literary circles. 'A Red, Red Rose' was one of 200 Scottish songs he wrote and collected for The Scots Musical Museum. Still honoured as Scotland's finest poet, Burns' birthday, 25 January, is remembered by Scots in a celebration, often marked by haggis and poetry, called Burns Night.*

The Taxi

When I go away from you

The world beats dead

Like a slackened drum.

I call out for you against the jutted stars

And shout into the ridges of the wind.

Streets coming fast,

One after the other,

Wedge you away from me,

And the lamps of the city prick my eyes

So that I can no longer see your face.

Why should I leave you,

To wound myself upon the sharp edges of the night?

Amy Lowell
1874–1925, b. USA

Amy Lowell was born into a prominent and wealthy New England family in 1874. The poets James Russell Lowell and Robert Lowell were family members, and Percy Lowell, the astronomer, was her brother. Lowell's love of books and poetry started at an early age. She was inspired to become a poet after reading Leigh Hunt's Imagination and Fancy and published her first poem in her late twenties. She wrote over 650 poems, was a great authority on John Keats and friend to a wide circle of writers.

So, We'll Go
No More a-Roving

So, we'll go no more a-roving
　　So late into the night,
Though the heart be still as loving,
　　And the moon be still as bright.

For the sword outwears its sheath,
　　And the soul wears out the breast,
And the heart must pause to breathe,
　　And love itself have rest.

Though the night was made for loving,
　　And the day returns too soon,
Yet we'll go no more a-roving
　　By the light of the moon.

Lord Byron
1788–1824, b. England

This poem was written in 1817, when Byron was enjoying a riotous and exhausting social life in Venice. Byron wrote the phrase 'so we'll go no more a-roving' in a letter to Thomas Moore, in which he admitted that his hedonistic lifestyle was wearing him out – '… yet I find "the sword wearing out the scabbard", though I have but just turned the corner of 29.'

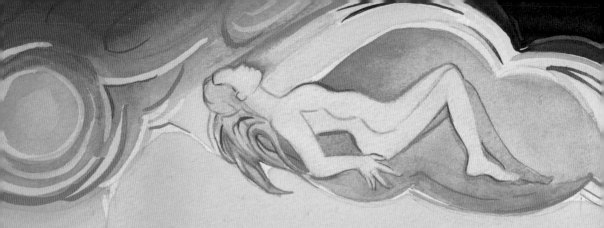

Sonnet 18

Shall I compare thee to a summer's day?

Thou art more lovely and more temperate:

Rough winds do shake the darling buds of May,

And summer's lease hath all too short a date;

Sometime too hot the eye of heaven shines,

And often is his gold complexion dimm'd,

And every fair from fair sometime declines,

By chance or nature's changing course untrimm'd:

But thy eternal summer shall not fade,

Nor lose possession of that fair thou ow'st,

Nor shall Death brag thou wand'rest in his shade,

When in eternal lines to time thou grow'st.

    So long as men can breathe or eyes can see,

    So long lives this, and this gives life to thee.

William Shakespeare

1564–1616, b. England

*S*hakespeare's cycle of 154 sonnets *was published in 1609, and probably written between 1592 and 1596. The first 126 seem to be addressed to a male friend, often urging him to marry and have children. The following 26 involve the seduction of the friend by a mysterious 'dark lady'. The two final sonnets are translations of Greek wit. Many scholars have failed to identify real people with the friend and the 'dark lady'.*

Answer to a Child's Question

Do you ask what the birds say?

The Sparrow, the Dove,

The Linnet and Thrush say, "I love and I love!"

In the winter they're silent – the wind is so strong;

What it says, I don't know, but it sings a loud song.

But green leaves, and blossoms,

and sunny warm weather,

And singing, and loving – all come back together.

But the Lark is so brimful of gladness and love,

The green fields below him, the blue sky above,

That he sings, and he sings; and for ever sings he –

"I love my Love, and my Love loves me!"

Samuel Taylor Coleridge
1772–1834, b. England

From 1797 to 1798 Coleridge lived in Somerset, near the poet William Wordsworth and his sister Dorothy. In 1789 the two men collaborated on a joint volume of poetry which featured Coleridge's Rime of the Ancient Mariner. *In the autumn of that year they travelled around Europe together with Coleridge studying German and philosophy. Coleridge returned to settle in Keswick in the Lake District and wrote this poem in 1802.*

Love and Age

I play'd with you 'mid cowslips blowing,

    When I was six and you were four;

When garlands weaving, flower-balls throwing,

    Were pleasures soon to please no more.

Through groves and meads, o'er grass and heather,

    With little playmates, to and fro,

We wander'd hand in hand together;

    But that was sixty years ago.

You grew a lovely roseate maiden,

    And still our early love was strong;

Still with no care our days were laden,

    They glided joyously along;

And I did love you very dearly,

    How dearly words want power to show;

I thought your heart was touch'd as nearly;

    But that was fifty years ago.

Then other lovers came around you,

    Your beauty grew from year to year,

And many a splendid circle found you

    The centre of its glittering sphere.

I saw you then, first vows forsaking,

    On rank and wealth your hand bestow;

O, then I thought my heart was breaking!—

But that was forty years ago.

And I lived on, to wed another:

    No cause she gave me to repine;

And when I heard you were a mother,

    I did not wish the children mine.

My own young flock, in fair progression,

    Made up a pleasant Christmas row:

My joy in them was past expression;

    But that was thirty years ago.

You grew a matron plump and comely,

    You dwelt in fashion's brightest blaze;

My earthly lot was far more homely;

    But I too had my festal days.

No merrier eyes have ever glisten'd

    Around the hearth-stone's wintry glow,

Than when my youngest child was christen'd;

    But that was twenty years ago.

Time pass'd. My eldest girl was married,

    And I am now a grandsire gray;

One pet of four years old I've carried

Among the wild-flower'd meads to play.
In our old fields of childish pleasure,
    Where now, as then, the cowslips blow,
She fills her basket's ample measure;
    And that is not ten years ago.

But though first love's impassion'd blindness
    Has pass'd away in colder light,
I still have thought of you with kindness,
    And shall do, till our last good-night.
The ever-rolling silent hours
    Will bring a time we shall not know,
When our young days of gathering flowers
    Will be an hundred years ago.

Thomas Love Peacock
1785–1866, b. England

Thomas Love Peacock was an English poet and novelist who satirized the cultural and political scene of his time. He ridiculed the well-known figures of the Romantic movement, like Wordsworth, Coleridge and Byron, but without hostile results. A meeting with Shelley in 1812 inspired his writing and a long friendship, which gave Peacock an introduction into the literary scene of the day.

His Mother's Wedding Ring

The ring so worn, as you behold,

So thin, so pale, is yet of gold:

The passion such it was to prove:

Worn with life's cares, love yet was love.

George Crabbe
1754–1832, b. England

*B*orn in Suffolk, Crabbe was apprenticed to a doctor in his early years but was determined to be a writer and left for London. In 1781 he took holy orders and became a curate, returning to live in Aldeburgh in Suffolk. His narrative style of poetry was much admired by Byron who called him 'nature's sternest painter yet the best'. He was a friend of the novelist Sir Walter Scott and Jane Austen's favourite poet.

Jenny Kissed Me

Jenny kissed me when we met,

Jumping from the chair she sat in;

Time, you thief! who love to get

Sweets into your list, put that in.

Say I'm weary, say I'm sad;

Say that health and wealth have

    miss'd me;

Say I'm growing old, but add –

Jenny kiss'd me.

Leigh Hunt
1784–1859, b. England

*I*t is said that the Jenny in question was Jane Carlyle, the wife of the English essayist Thomas Carlyle. Hunt had just recovered from a bout of influenza and went to tell the Carlyles the news. Jane, in an uncharacteristic move, jumped up from her chair and kissed him.

To Celia

Drink to me only with thine eyes,

And I will pledge with mine;

Or leave a kiss but in the cup

And I'll not look for wine.

The thirst that from the soul doth rise

Doth ask a drink divine;

But might I of Jove's nectar sup,

I would not change for thine.

I sent thee late a rosy wreath,

Not so much honouring thee

As giving it a hope that there

It could not withered be;

But thou thereon didst only breathe,

And sent'st it back to me;

Since when it grows, and smells, I swear,

Not of itself but thee!

Ben Jonson
1572–1637, b. England

Ben Jonson was one of a group of writers, including Shakespeare, John Donne, Beaumont and Fletcher, who gathered at the Mermaid Tavern in Cheapside, London. Jonson was a very volatile man and this was reflected in his life and his plays and poetry.

He spent time in prison for involvement in a satire in 1597 and was tried at the Old Bailey for murder, having killed a fellow actor in a duel. He influenced nearly all the writers of the 17th century and made a lasting impression on English drama.

from The Bible

I am the rose of Sharon,
and the lily of the valleys.

As the lily among thorns,
so is my love among the daughters.

As the apple tree among the trees of the wood,
so is my beloved among the sons.
I sat down under his shadow with great delight,
and his fruit was sweet to my taste.
He brought me to the banqueting house,
and his banner over me was love.
Stay me with flagons, comfort me with apples:
for I am sick of love.

His left hand is under my head,

and his right hand doth embrace me.

I charge you, O ye daughters of Jerusalem,

by the roes, and by the hinds of the field...

that ye stir not up, nor awake my love...

till he please.

? King Solomon

circa 928BC

Song of Songs 2: 1–7

*T*he Song of Songs *celebrates love through a dialogue between two people – the lover (shown above in italics) and the beloved. King Solomon was known for his wealth, writings and* wisdom. *As well as being credited as the author of the Song of Songs, he is also thought to have written 1005 other songs and 3000 proverbs.*

Appeal

Daphnis dearest, wherefore weave me

Webs of lies lest truth should grieve me?

I could pardon much, believe me:

Dower me, Daphnis, or bereave me,

Kiss me, kill me, love me, leave me,

Damn me, dear, but don't deceive me!

Edith Nesbit
1858–1924, b. England

*E*dith Nesbit was born in London, and studied in England, France and Germany. She published her first poems at the age of 17. Her literary output was tremendous and she was the author of over 40 children's books including Five Children and It, published in 1902, and The Railway Children, published in 1906. She was married twice and had a vast circle of friends, including George Bernard Shaw and H G Wells.

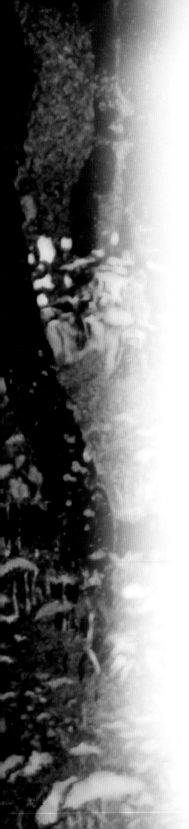

My Delight and Thy Delight

My delight and thy delight
Walking, like two angels white,
In the gardens of the night:

My desire and thy desire
Twining to a tongue of fire,
Leaping live, and laughing higher:

Thro' the everlasting strife
In the mystery of life.
Love from whom the world begun,
Hath the secret of the sun.

Love can tell, and love alone,
Whence the million stars were strewn,
Why each atom knows its own,
How, in spite of woe and death,

Gay is life, and sweet is breath:

This he taught us, this we knew,

Happy in his science true,

Hand in hand as we stood

'Neath the shadows of the wood,

Heart to heart as we lay

In the dawning of the day.

Robert Bridges
1844–1930, b. England

Robert Bridges was educated at Eton and Oxford and went on to study medicine at St Bartholomew's Hospital, which he practised until 1882. His early shorter poems contain beautiful descriptions of nature. As well as much prose, he published poems, plays and anthologies. Bridges was one of the founders of the Society of English and he was appointed Poet Laureate in 1913.

And When Love Speaks

And when Love speaks, the voice of all the gods

Make heaven drowsy with the harmony.

An extract from Love's Labour's Lost,
William Shakespeare
1564–1616, b. England

*L*ove's Labour's Lost, *one of William Shakespeare's earlier works, is a comedy. Shakespeare's career bridged the reigns of two monarchs, Elizabeth I* (ruled 1558–1603) *and James I (ruled 1603–25) and he was a favourite of both. James I granted Shakespeare's company the status of king's players.*

You Smiled

You smiled, you spoke and I believed,
By every word and smile – deceived.

Another man would hope no more;
Nor hope I – what I hoped before.

But let not this last wish be vain;
Deceive, deceive me once again!

Walter Savage Landor
1775–1864, b. England

Walter Savage Landor was an irascible character and consequently had an eventful life. He had been sent down from Oxford University and went to live in Italy after being sued for libel. After 20 years he returned to live in Bath but later went back to Italy where he was helped by Robert Browning. Landor wrote poetry throughout his life. His friend Charles Dickens based the character of Boythorn in Bleak House on Landor.

One Day I Wrote Her Name

One day I wrote her name upon the strand,

But came the waves and washed it away:

Again I wrote it with a second hand,

But came the tide and made my pains his prey.

"Vain man," said she, "that dost in vain essay

A mortal thing so to immortalize;

For I myself shall like to this decay,

And eke my name be wiped out likewise."

"Not so," quoth I; "let baser things devise

To lie in dust, but you shall live by fame;

My verse your virtues rare shall eternize,

And in the heavens write your glorious name:

Where, whenas Death shall all the world subdue,

Our love shall live, and later life renew."

Edmund Spenser
1552?–99, b. England

*T*he Elizabethan poet Edmund Spenser was born in London. After attending Cambridge University, he lived in the North of England and then took up an appointment in Ireland. Spenser's greatest work is The Faerie Queene, *an allegory of good and evil. Despite being known to his contemporaries as the "prince of poets", he died in penury and was buried in Westminster Abbey.*

Annie Laurie

Maxwelton's hills are bonnie
Where early falls the dew
And 'twas there that Annie Laurie
Gived me her promise true.
Gived me her promise true
Which ne'er forgot shall be
And for bonnie Annie Laurie
I'd lay me down and die.

Her brow is like the snow drift,
Her throat is like the swan,
Her face, it is the fairest
That e'er the sun shone on.
That e'er the sun shone on
And dark blue are her eyes
And for bonnie Annie Laurie
I'd lay me down and die.

Like dew on the daisy lyin'
Is the fall of her fairy feet
And like winds in summer sighing
Her voice is low and sweet.

Her voice is low and sweet
And she's all the world to me
And for bonnie Annie Laurie
I'd lay me down and die.

William Douglas
1672–1748, b. Scotland

William Douglas wrote the love poem 'Annie Laurie' around 1700. He composed the verses having fallen in love with a celebrated beauty called Anne Laurie. They did not marry but the verses endured and an accompanying tune was written later by Lady John Scott and published in 1835, making it a great favourite.

EVENTS

***

*Major events and anniversaries,
whether birthdays, Christmas, New Year's Eve,
Bonfire Night or battles, have inspired some great
poems. From Clement Clarke Moore's vivid
'The Night Before Christmas', and the joyous
'A Birthday' of Christina Rossetti, to the battlefield
regrets of John McCrae's 'In Flanders Fields' and
the heart-warming words of 'Auld Lang Syne', the
poems in this section provide insights to many
significant dates in the calendar.*

The Night before Christmas

'Twas the night before Christmas, when all through
the house
Not a creature was stirring, not even a mouse;
The stockings were hung by the chimney with care,
In hopes that St Nicholas soon would be there;

The children were nestled all snug in their beds,

While visions of sugar plums danced in their heads;

And mamma in her w'kerchief, and I in my cap,

Had just settled our brains for a long winter's nap,

When out on the lawn there arose such a clatter,

I sprang from the bed to see what was the matter.

Away to the window I flew like a flash,

Tore open the shutters and threw up the sash.

The moon on the breast of the new-fallen snow

Gave the lustre of midday to objects below,

When, what to my wondering eyes should appear,

But a miniature sleigh, and eight tiny reindeer,

With a little old driver, so lively and quick,

I knew in a moment it must be St Nick.

More rapid than eagles his coursers they came,

And he whistled, and shouted, and called them

    by name:

'Now, Dasher! now, Dancer! now, Prancer and Vixen!

On, Comet! on, Cupid! on, Donner and Blitzen!

To the top of the porch! to the top of the wall!

Now dash away! dash away! dash away all!'

As dry leaves that before the wild hurricane fly,

When they meet with an obstacle, mount to the sky,

So up to the house-top the coursers they flew,

With the sleigh full of toys, and St Nicholas too.

And then, in a twinkling, I heard on the roof

The prancing and pawing of each little hoof.

As I drew in my head, and was turning around,

Down the chimney St Nicholas came with a bound.

He was dressed all in fur, from his head to his foot,

And his clothes were all tarnished with ashes

    and soot;

A bundle of toys he had flung on his back,

And he looked like a pedlar just opening his pack.

His eyes – how they twinkled, his dimples how merry!

His cheeks were like roses, his nose like a cherry!

His droll little mouth was drawn up like a bow,

And the beard of his chin was as white as the snow;

The stump of a pipe he held tight in his teeth,

And the smoke it encircled his head like a wreath;
He had a broad face and a little round belly,
That shook, when he laughed, like a bowlful of jelly.
He was chubby and plump, a right jolly old elf,
And I laughed when I saw him, in spite of myself;

A wink of his eyes and a twist of his head,
Soon gave me to know I had nothing to dread;
He spoke not a word, but went straight to his work,
And filled all the stockings, then turned with a jerk,
And laying his finger aside of his nose,
And giving a nod, up the chimney he rose;
He sprang to his sleigh, to his team gave a whistle,
And away they all flew like the down of a thistle.
But I heard him exclaim, ere he drove out of sight,
'Happy Christmas to all, and to all a good night.'

Clement Clarke Moore
1779–1863, b. USA

A distinguished New York professor of Bible studies, Moore wrote this poem in 1822 for his six children. It was published anonymously in the Troy Sentinel *on December 23 1823 and was an instant success, but Moore* did not acknowledge authorship until it appeared in The New York Book of Poetry (1837). *Our modern-day idea of Father Christmas comes from the enduring popularity of this poem.*

A Birthday

My heart is like a singing bird

    Whose nest is in a water'd shoot;

My heart is like an apple-tree

    Whose boughs are bent with thickset fruit;

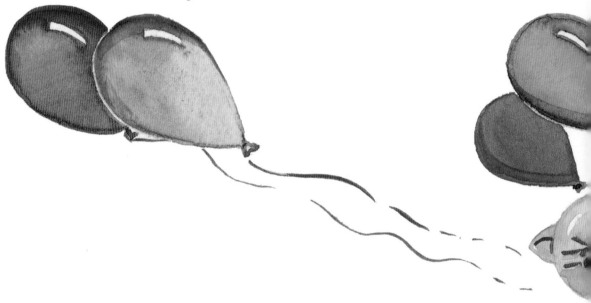

My heart is like a rainbow shell

    That paddles in a halcyon sea;

My heart is gladder than all these

    Because my love is come to me.

Raise me a dais of silk and down;

    Hang it with vair and purple dyes;

Carve it in doves and pomegranates,

    And peacocks with a hundred eyes;

Work it in gold and silver grapes,

    In leaves and silver fleurs-de-lys;

Because the birthday of my life

    Is come, my love is come to me.

Christina Rossetti
1830–94, b. England

Christina Rossetti's family were devoted to literature, music and art. Christina composed poetry from an early age and frequently modelled for her painter brother, Dante Gabriel Rossetti. Her nursery rhymes, verses, ballads and sonnets are often haunted by a wistful melancholy. The overwhelming joy expressed in 'A Birthday' suggests that, while it can be read as either a devotional or a secular poem, it was more likely intended as an expression of Christina's devout religious faith.

Hot Cross Buns!

Hot cross buns! Hot cross buns!

One a penny, two a penny.

Hot cross buns!

Hot cross buns! Hot cross buns!

If ye have no daughters,

Give them to your sons.

Traditional rhyme

The rhyme about hot cross buns is well known in the playground. It celebrates the small spicy fruit cakes decorated with a white cross which are traditionally sold during Easter.

They have a religious significance – of the resurrection of Jesus Christ following his death on the cross in the Easter Christian festival.

Easter Poem

Hark! how the children shrill and high

Hosanna cry,

Their joys provoke the distant sky,

Where thrones and seraphims reply,

And their own angels shine and sing

In a bright ring:

Such young, sweet mirth

Makes heaven and earth

Join in a joyful symphony.

Henry Vaughan
1622–95, b. Wales

*H*enry Vaughan was born in Wales and studied at Jesus College, Oxford. He was recalled home at the outbreak of the English Civil War. He was one of the group of Metaphysical poets, which included John Donne and Andrew Marvell, and his poetry showed a delight in the natural world. His work was an influence on the poetry of the 20th century.

from The American Flag

When freedom, from her mountain height
Unfurled her standard to the air,
She tore the azure robe of night
And set the stars of glory there.
She mingled with its gorgeous dyes
The milky baldric of the skies,
Then from his mansion in the sun
She called her eagle-bearer down
And gave into his mighty hand
The symbol of her chosen land.

Joseph Rodman Drake
1795–1820, b. USA

*T*he American poet and satirist Joseph Rodman Drake was born in New York. Under the name of "the Croakers" he and his friend Fitz-Greene Halleck wrote a series of light satirical verses for the New York Evening Post. He is probably best known for his patriotic classic 'The American Flag'. Drake died of tuberculosis at the early age of 25 .

Making Jack o' Lanterns

Just take a golden pumpkin
Of quite the largest size,
Cut all 'round the stem, just so,
Scrape out the inside below,

And cut two holes for eyes.

And now fix a nose beneath,

And such a great big mouth with teeth,

And you've a Jack o' Lantern!

Then fix a tallow candle,

Just big enough to light,

And when it flickers, see him blink,

And when it flares up, see him wink

And smile so broad and bright.

This is the jolliest sort of a fellow,

With cheery face so round and yellow,

This funny Jack o' Lantern.

Anonymous

Carving Jack o' Lanterns is a Hallowe'en custom dating back to ancient Ireland. The first lanterns were made of hollowed-out beets or turnips.

When Irish immigrants arrived in the United States they took their custom with them but used the bright orange-coloured pumpkins instead.

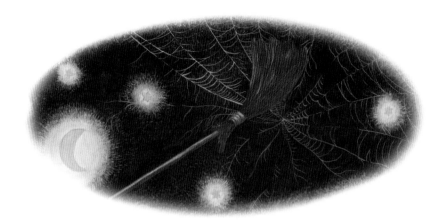

Litany For Hallowe'en

From ghoulies and ghosties,

Long-leggedy beasties,

And things that go bump in the night,

Good Lord, deliver us.

Anonymous

Hallowe'en is celebrated on October 31, marking the end of the summer and the harvest and the beginning of the winter. Nowadays it is a time for making Jack o' Lanterns from scooped-out pumpkins, lit from inside to make ghoulish faces, and for trick or treating – going from house to house in the neighbourhood getting gifts of sweets. Hallowe'en dates back for centuries and takes its name from All Hallows Eve.

I Sing of Brooks

I sing of brooks, of blossoms, birds, and bowers:

Of April, May, or June, and July flowers.

I sing of Maypoles, Hock-carts, wassails, wakes,

Of bridegrooms, brides, and of the bridal cakes.

Robert Herrick
1591–1674, b. England

The clergyman and poet Robert Herrick was born in London in 1591. He wrote poetry from an early age, attended Cambridge University and soon became a well-known poet mixing in literary circles. He was given a living by Charles I in a remote parish in Devon and wrote much of his work there. He was a distinguished lyric poet and some of his love poetry, such as 'Gather Ye Rosebuds', is still much loved.

In Flanders Fields

In Flanders fields the poppies blow
Between the crosses, row on row,
That mark our place; and in the sky
The larks, still bravely singing, fly
Scarce heard amid the guns below.

We are the Dead. Short days ago
We lived, felt dawn, saw sunset glow,
Loved and were loved, and now we lie
In Flanders fields.

Take up our quarrel with the foe:
To you from failing hands we throw
The torch; be yours to hold it high.
If ye break with us who die
We shall not sleep, though poppies grow
In Flanders fields.

Major John McCrae
1872–1918, b. Canada

The poem 'In Flanders Fields' was written during the Battle of Ypres in spring 1915. The Canadian Army physician John McCrae was working in a dressing station treating injured men. After a run of 17 days McCrae sat on the rear step of an ambulance and penned this famous poem from World War I. McCrae threw the poem to one side but it was rescued by a fellow officer who submitted it to Punch for publication. John McCrae died while on active duty in 1918.

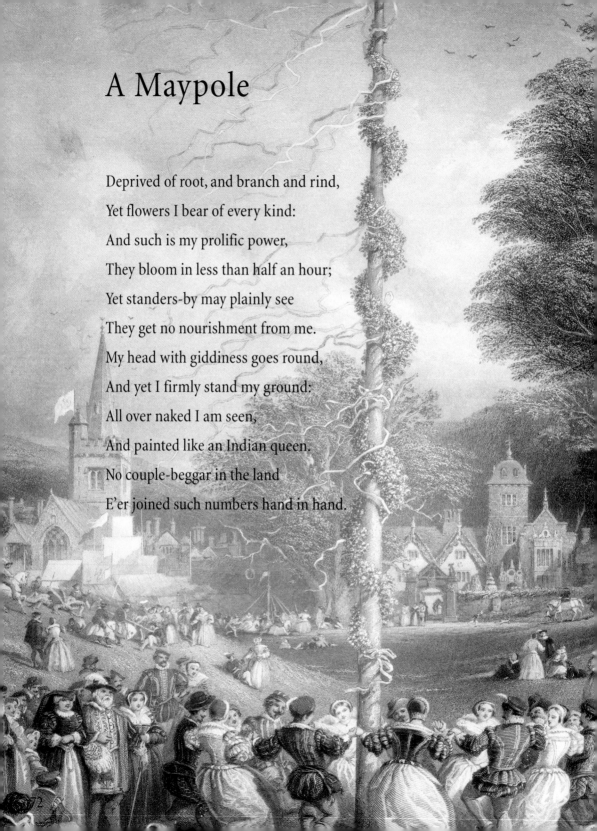

A Maypole

Deprived of root, and branch and rind,
Yet flowers I bear of every kind:
And such is my prolific power,
They bloom in less than half an hour;
Yet standers-by may plainly see
They get no nourishment from me.
My head with giddiness goes round,
And yet I firmly stand my ground:
All over naked I am seen,
And painted like an Indian queen.
No couple-beggar in the land
E'er joined such numbers hand in hand.

I joined them fairly with a ring;

Nor can our parson blame the thing.

And though no marriage words are spoke,

They part not till the ring is broke;

Yet hypocrite fanatics cry,

I'm but an idol raised on high;

And once a weaver in our town,

A damned Cromwellian, knocked me down.

I lay a prisoner twenty years,

And then the jovial cavaliers

To their old post restored all three –

I mean the church, the king, and me

Jonathan Swift
1667–1745, b. Ireland

*M*ay Day was a pagan festival *celebrating the first spring planting. Dancing round the maypole has long been a traditional celebration of May Day. A dozen or so people, holding hands and each holding on to a ribbon attached to the top of the pole, weave in and out dancing to music and plaiting and unplaiting the ribbons.*

'Twas the Night of Thanksgiving

'Twas the night of Thanksgiving,

    but I just couldn't sleep.

I tried counting backwards, I tried counting sheep.

The leftovers beckoned – the dark meat and white,

    but I fought the temptation with all of my might.

Tossing and turning with anticipation,

    the thought of a snack became infatuation.

So, I raced to the kitchen,

    flung open the door

and gazed at the fridge,

full of goodies galore.

I gobbled up turkey and buttered potatoes,

pickles and carrots, beans and tomatoes.

I felt myself swelling so plump and so round,

till all of a sudden, I rose off the ground.

I crashed through the ceiling,

floating into the sky

With a mouthful of pudding and a handful of pie.

But, I managed to yell as I soared past the trees...

happy eating to all – pass the cranberries, please!

Anonymous

Thanksgiving Day in the United States dates from the time in the 17th century when the Pilgrim settlers in Massachusetts celebrated their successful and plentiful autumn harvest. The governor, William Bradford, proclaimed a day of thanksgiving to be shared by neighbouring colonists and Native American Indians. It was not until 1863 that a national day of thanksgiving was instituted and on the fourth Thursday of every November, traditional food and family gatherings are celebrated.

Hurrahing in Harvest

Summer ends now; now, barbarous in beauty, the stooks arise
    Around; up above, what wind-walks! what lovely behaviour
    Of silk-sack clouds! has wilder, wilful-wavier
Meal-drift moulded ever and melted across skies?

I walk, I lift up, I lift up heart, eyes,
    Down all that glory in the heavens to glean our Saviour;
    And, éyes, heárt, what looks, what lips yet gave you a
Rapturous love's greeting of realer, of rounder replies?

And the azurous hung hills are his world-wielding shoulder

    Majestic – as a stallion stalwart, very-violet-sweet! –

These things, these things were here and but the beholder

    Wanting; which two when they once meet,

The heart réars wíngs bold and bolder

    And hurls for him, O half hurls earth for him off under his feet.

Gerard Manley Hopkins
1844–89, b. England

Hopkins had thoughts of becoming a painter–poet like Gabriel Dante Rossetti and was greatly influenced by aesthetic figures like John Ruskin and poets like Christina Rossetti and George Herbert. But instead he worked as a preacher, parish priest and professor of Latin and Greek and considered his poetry as coming second to his other duties. His poetry was not so well known in his lifetime and the first collection was published in 1918.

Auld Lang Syne
(Old Long Ago)

Should old acquaintance be forgot,
And never brought to mind;
Should old acquaintance be forgot,
And days of old lang syne.

    For old lang syne, my dear,
    For old lang syne,
    We'll take a cup of kindness yet,
    For old lang syne.

We two have run about the hills,
And pulled the daisies fine.
We've wandered many a weary foot,
Since old lang syne.

We two have paddled in the burn [stream],
From morning sun till dine,
But seas between us broad have roared,
Since old lang syne.

And here's a hand my trusty friend,

And put your hand in mine.

We'll take a right good willie-waught [drink],

For old lang syne.

And surely you'll lift up your glass,

For surely I'll lift mine,

And we'll drink a cup of kindness yet,

For old lang syne.

? Robert Burns
1759–96, b. Scotland
translated by William Curran

Translated from the old Scottish dialect, 'Auld Lang Syne' is traditionally sung at the stroke of midnight on New Year's Eve and in Scotland on Burns Night, January 25, to celebrate the life of the author and poet Robert Burns. It is a song about love and friendship in times past and is popularly thought to have been written by Burns.

The Oxen

Christmas Eve, and twelve of the clock.
'Now they are all on their knees,'
An elder said as we sat in a flock
By the embers in hearthside ease.

We pictured the meek mild creatures where
They dwelt in their strawy pen,
Nor did it occur to one of us there
To doubt they were kneeling then.

So fair a fancy few would weave

In these years! Yet, I feel,

If someone said on Christmas Eve,

'Come; see the oxen kneel,

'In the lonely barton by yonder coomb

Our childhood used to know,'

I should go with him in the gloom,

Hoping it might be so.

Thomas Hardy
1840–1928, b. England

An architect by profession, Thomas Hardy made his fame and fortune as a novelist. However, he always wrote poetry too, believing it to be superior to fiction. When Tess of the D'Urbervilles (1891) and Jude the Obscure (1895) caused outrage, Hardy gave up writing novels and concentrated on his poems. Many remember cherished moments in the past, often associated with his first wife. 'The Oxen' is a tender memory of the strong religious faith of his childhood.

Father's Day

Walk a little slower, Daddy,

Said a little child so small.

I'm following in your footsteps

And I don't want to fall.

Sometimes your steps are very fast,

Sometimes they are hard to see;

So, walk a little slower, Daddy,

For you are leading me.

Someday when I'm all grown up,

You're what I want to be;

Then I will have a little child

Who'll want to follow me.

And I would want to lead just right,

And know that I was true;

So walk a little slower, Daddy,

For I must follow you.

Author unknown

*W*hich grown up could not be affected by the plea 'Walk a little slower, Daddy'? The poem has come into popular use around the annual Father's Day celebrations, in the United States and Europe.

Parted

Farewell to one now silenced quite,
Sent out of hearing, out of sight,–
My friend of friends, whom I shall miss,
He is not banished, though, for this,–
Nor he, nor sadness, nor delight.
Though I shall talk with him no more,
A low voice sounds upon the shore.
He must not watch my resting-place,
But who shall drive a mournful face
From the sad winds about my door?
I shall not hear his voice complain,
But who shall stop the patient rain?
His tears must not disturb my heart,
But who shall change the years and part
The world from any thought of pain?

Although my life is left so dim,

The morning crowns the mountain-rim;

Joy is not gone from summer skies,

Nor innocence from children's eyes,

And all of these things are part of him.

He is not banished, for the showers

Yet wake this green warm earth of ours.

How can the summer but be sweet?

I shall not have him at my feet,

And yet my feet are on the flowers.

Alice Meynell

1847–1922, b. England

A lice Meynell was an English poet and essayist. She had a rather bohemian upbringing, some of it in Italy. Meynell was a committed Roman Catholic and wrote much on religious subjects and contributed to her husband's paper Merry England. Her work was much admired by many of her contemporaries such as Tennyson and Walter de la Mer.

Roses Are Red

Roses are red.

Violets are blue.

Sugar is sweet.

And so are you.

Traditional rhyme

*V*alentine's Day is celebrated on February 14 each year and is the day when lovers exchange gifts. The origins of the patron saint St Valentine are shrouded in mystery.

Commercial valentines were introduced in the 1800s and the verse 'Roses Are Red' is probably one of the best-known love poems.

Bonfire Night

Remember remember the fifth of November

Gunpowder, treason and plot.

I see no reason why gunpowder, treason

Should ever be forgot...

Traditional rhyme

The old rhyme reminding us to remember the fifth of November dates back to the reign of King James I. In 1605 a group of conspirators stored barrels of gunpowder in a cellar beneath the House of Lords hoping to blow up the king and his supporters. Someone betrayed the group and the plot was foiled. Celebrations are still held each year with bonfires and burning guys, named after Guy Fawkes, one of the group.

DISTANT LANDS

'I met a traveller from an antique land' are
the opening words of Shelley's 'Ozymandias'.
Instantly we are intrigued and need to go on – just
like the travellers and explorers in this selection.
Robert Browning yearns for an English spring,
Coleridge's ancient mariner, becalmed in a
sweltering ocean, cries out for drinking water,
while Stephen Crane takes a philosophical view
from a metaphorical mountain top.

Ozymandias

I met a traveller from an antique land
Who said: Two vast and trunkless legs of stone
Stand in the desert … Near them, on the sand,
Half sunk, a shattered visage lies, whose frown,
And wrinkled lip, and sneer of cold command,
Tell that its sculptor well those passions read

Which yet survive, stamped on these lifeless things,

The hand that mocked them and the heart that fed;

And on the pedestal these words appear:

'My name is OZYMANDIAS, king of kings:

Look on my works, ye Mighty, and despair!'

Nothing beside remains. Round the decay

Of that colossal wreck, boundless and bare

The lone and level sands stretch far away.

Percy Bysshe Shelley

1792–1822, b. England

Bullied as a boy, Shelley grew up to ignore social convention. He dressed unusually, was a vegetarian and atheist, eloped with a 16-year-old, then left her for Mary Godwin (author of Frankenstein). Twice he tried to set up a community of 'free spirits'.

'Ozymandias' describes how a dictator's efforts to be remembered for ever have been beaten by time and nature. (Ozymandias was another name for the Egyptian pharaoh Rameses II, who built a huge tomb in the shape of a Sphinx.)

Home-thoughts, from Abroad

O to be in England

Now that April's there,

And whoever wakes in England

Sees, some morning, unaware,

That the lowest boughs and the brushwood sheaf

Round the elm-tree bole are in tiny leaf,

While the chaffinch sings on the orchard bough

In England – now!

And after April, when May follows,

And the whitethroat builds, and all the swallows!

Hark, where my blossom'd pear-tree in the hedge

Leans to the field and scatters on the clover

Blossoms and dewdrops – at the bent spray's edge –

That's the wise thrush; he sings each song twice over

Lest you should think he never could recapture

The first fine careless rapture!

And though the fields look rough with hoary dew,

All will be gay when noontide wakes anew

The buttercups, the little children's dower

– Far brighter than this gaudy melon-flower!

Robert Browning
1812–89, b. England

Robert Browning spent much of his childhood reading in his father's massive library of 6000 books, and he wrote his first volume of poems at the age of 12. He had limited success early on in his career, and after trips to Russia and Italy, he eloped to Italy in 1846 with the poet Elizabeth Barrett. The couple lived first in Pisa, then in Florence, Browning only returning home to England after Elizabeth's death in 1861.

from The Rime of the Ancient Mariner

'The Sun now rose upon the right:
Out of the sea came he,
Still hid in mist, and on the left
Went down into the sea.

And the good south wind still blew behind,
But no sweet bird did follow,
Nor any day for food or play
Came to the mariners' hollo!

And I had done a hellish thing,
And it would work 'em woe:
For all averred, I had killed the bird
That made the breeze to blow.
Ah wretch! said they, the bird to slay,
That made the breeze to blow!

Down dropt the breeze, the sails dropt
    down,
'Twas sad as sad could be;
And we did speak only to break
The silence of the sea!

All in a hot and copper sky,

The bloody Sun, at noon,

Right up above the mast did stand,

No bigger than the Moon.

Day after day, day after day,

We stuck, nor breath nor motion;

As idle as a painted ship

Upon a painted ocean.

Water, water, every where,
And all the boards did shrink;
Water, water every where,
Nor any drop to drink.

The very deep did rot: O Christ!
That ever this should be!
Yea, slimy things did crawl with legs
Upon the slimy sea.

About, about, in reel and rout
The death-fires danced at night;
The water, like a witch's oils,
Burnt green and blue and white.

And some in dreams assurèd were
Of the Spirit that plagued us so;
Nine fathom deep he had followed us
From the land of mist and snow.

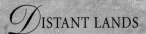

And every tongue, through utter drought,

Was withered at the root;

We could not speak, no more than if

We had been choked with soot.

Ah! well a-day! What evil looks

Had I from old and young!

Instead of the cross, the Albatross

About my neck was hung.'

Samuel Taylor Coleridge
1772–1834, b. England

This great Romantic poem tells the story of an old sea-dog, whose ship once got ice-bound near the South Pole. An albatross appears and the ship floats free, but when the sailor shoots the bird, a curse falls upon the vessel and it is becalmed under the burning Equator sun. A skeleton ship approaches and all the crew die except the narrator. It is only when the mariner finds the kindness to bless the slimy watersnakes in the rotting sea that the ship is finally able to turn for home.

Travel

I should like to rise and go
Where the golden apples grow;
Where below another sky
Parrot islands anchored lie,
And, watched by cockatoos and goats,
Lonely Crusoes building boats;
Where in sunshine reaching out
Eastern cities, miles about,
Are with mosque and minaret
Among sandy gardens set,
And the rich goods from near and far
Hang for sale in the bazaar;
Where the Great Wall round China goes,
And on one side the desert blows,
And with the voice and bell and drum,
Cities on the other hum;
Where are forests hot as fire,
Wide as England, tall as a spire,
Full of apes and cocoa-nuts
And the negro hunters' huts;

Where the knotty crocodile
Lies and blinks in the Nile,
And the red flamingo flies
Hunting fish before his eyes;
Where in jungles near and far,
Man-devouring tigers are,
Lying close and giving ear
Lest the hunt be drawing near,
Or a comer-by be seen
Swinging in the palanquin;
Where among the desert sands
Some deserted city stands,
All its children, sweep and prince,
Grown to manhood ages since,
Not a foot in street or house,
Not a stir of child or mouse,
And when kindly falls the night,
In all the town no spark of light.
There I'll come when I'm a man
With a camel caravan;

Light a fire in the gloom

Of some dusty dining-room;

See the pictures on the walls,

Heroes fights and festivals;

And in a corner find the toys

Of the old Egyptian boys.

Robert Louis Stevenson
1850–94, b. Scotland

Robert Louis Stevenson suffered from ill-health all his life and travelled extensively to warm climates. His output was considerable and much of Stevensons' writing recalls his own experiences of different countries. This poem richly evokes images of exotic lands. He eventually settled with his family in Samoa in the South Seas.

The Slave's Lament

It was in sweet Senegal

That my foes did me enthral

For the lands of Virginia, –ginia, O!

Torn from that lovely shore,

And must never see it more,

And alas! I am weary, weary, O!

All on that charming coast

Is no bitter snow and frost,

Like the lands of Virginia, –ginia, O!

There streams for ever flow,

And the flowers for ever blow,

And alas! I am weary, weary, O!

The burden I must bear,

While the cruel scourge I fear,

In the lands of Virginia, –ginia, O!

And I think on friends most dear

With the bitter, bitter tear,

And alas! I am weary, weary, O!

Robert Burns
1759–96, b. Scotland

Slaves were transported to the United States to work in the developing cotton, sugarcane and tobacco industries. Burns evokes a sense of longing for home in this poem and the Senegalese slave's new life in the tobacco-rich plantations of Virginia. It was not until 1865 that Congress ratified the 13th Amendment to the US Constitution, which abolished slavery, over 70 years after Burns died.

Impression du Voyage

The sea was sapphire coloured, and the sky
Burned like a heated opal through the air,
We hoisted sail; the wind was blowing fair
For the blue lands that to the eastward lie.
From the steep prow I marked with quickening eye
Zakynthos, every olive grove and creek,
Ithaca's cliff, Lycaon's snowy peak,
And all the flower-strewn hills of Arcady.
The flapping of the sail against the mast,
The ripple of the water on the side,
The ripple of girls' laughter at the stern,
The only sounds: – when 'gan the West to burn,
And a red sun upon the seas to ride,
I stood upon the soil of Greece at last!

Oscar Wilde
1854–1900, b. Ireland

*I*rish-born Oscar Wilde was a leading figure in the Aesthetic movement, with a great reputation as a humorist and wit. His elegant social comedies such as Lady Windermere's Fan *and* An Ideal Husband *are still popular* today. He travelled to the United States on a very successful lecture tour and lived in London and Paris. His poem 'Impression du Voyage' paints a very evocative picture of a journey to the Greek islands.

107

from War is Kind and Other Lines

When the prophet, a complacent fat man,

Arrived at the mountain-top,

He cried: 'Woe to my knowledge!

I intended to see good white lands

And bad black lands,

But the scene is grey.'

Stephen Crane
1871–1900, b. USA

The American-born writer Stephen Crane came from a large New York family. He lived the life of a penniless down-and-out artist and writer, and became known as a social critic and realist as well as a poet and journalist.

As a journalist Crane covered both the Greco-Turkish and Spanish-American Wars. His novel The Red Badge of Courage, *published in 1895, deals vividly with the American Civil War.*

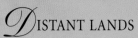

from Leaves of Grass

Book VI Salut du Monde

I see the long river-stripes of the earth,

I see the Amazon and the Paraguay,

I see the four great rivers of China, the Amour,

    the Yellow River, the Yiang-tse, and the Pearl,

I see where the Seine flows, and where the Danube,

    the Loire, the Rhone, and the Guadalquiver flow,

I see the windings of the Volga, the Dnieper, the Oder,

I see the Tuscan going down the Arno, and the Venetian

    along the Po,

I see the Greek seaman sailing out of Egina bay.

Walt Whitman
1819–92, b. USA

*W*alt Whitman was a voracious reader and in his early life was well-acquainted with Homer, Dante, Shakespeare and Scott. He also knew the Bible thoroughly. He began working in teaching but changed to journalism, and developed a style of poetry that has made him one of America's favourite poets. Whitman was fond of music and his poems often resonate with a musical quality.

The Soldier

If I should die, think only this of me:
　　That there's some corner of a foreign field
That is for ever England. There shall be
　　In that rich earth a richer dust concealed;
A dust whom England bore, shaped, made aware,
　　Gave, once her flowers to love, her ways to roam,
A body of England's, breathing English air,
　　Washed by the rivers, blessed by the suns of home.

And think, this heart, all evil shed away,
　　A pulse in the eternal mind, no less
　　　　Gives somewhere back the thoughts by
　　　　　　England given;
Her sights and sounds; dreams happy as her day;
　　And laughter, learnt of friends; and gentleness,
　　　　In hearts a peace, under an English heaven.

Rupert Brooke
1887–1915, b. England

*R*upert Brooke served in the RNVR during World War I. After taking part in the Antwerp expedition of 1914, he wrote 'The Soldier' as one of five 'War Sonnets'. The poems were published early in 1915 in New Numbers and received rapturously by the public. Brooke died of blood poisoning the same year, on a French hospital ship in the Aegean Sea. The posthumous publication of 1914 and Other Poems firmly established him as the nation's poet of war.

Kubla Khan

In Xanadu did Kubla Khan
A stately pleasure-dome decree:
Where Alph, the sacred river, ran
Through caverns measureless to man
Down to a sunless sea.
So twice five miles of fertile ground
With walls and towers were girdled round:
And here were gardens bright with sinuous rills,
Where blossomed many an incense-bearing tree;
And here were forests ancient as the hills,
Enfolding sunny spots of greenery.

But oh! that deep romantic chasm which slanted

Down the green hill athwart a cedarn cover!

A savage place! as holy and enchanted

As e'er beneath a waning moon was haunted

By woman wailing for her demon-lover!

And from this chasm, with ceaseless turmoil seething,

As if this earth in fast thick pants were breathing,

A mighty fountain momently was forced:

Amid whose swift half-intermitted burst

Huge fragments vaulted like rebounding hail,

Or chaffy grain beneath the thresher's flail:

And 'mid these dancing rocks at once and ever

It flung up momently the sacred river.

Five miles meandering with a mazy motion
Through wood and dale the sacred river ran,
Then reached the caverns measureless to man,
And sank in tumult to a lifeless ocean:
And 'mid this tumult Kubla heard from far
Ancestral voices prophesying war!

    The shadow of the dome of pleasure
    Floated midway on the waves;
    Where was heard the mingled measure
    From the fountain and the caves.
It was a miracle of rare device,
A sunny pleasure-dome with caves of ice!

A damsel with a dulcimer

In a vision once I saw:

It was an Abyssinian maid,

And on her dulcimer she played,

Singing of Mount Abora,

Could I revive within me

Her symphony and song,

To such a deep delight 'twould win me,

That with music loud and long,

I would build that dome in air,

That sunny dome! those caves of ice!

And all who heard should see them there,

And all should cry, Beware! Beware!

His flashing eyes, his floating hair!

Weave a circle round him thrice,

And close your eyes with holy dread,

For he on honey-dew hath fed,

And drunk the milk of Paradise.

Samuel Taylor Coleridge
1772–1834, b. England

Samuel Taylor Coleridge lived to see many amazing scientific discoveries and also the French Revolution, when the ordinary people overthrew the ruling nobility. It must have seemed as if anything was possible, if only you had enough imagination and energy.

Kubla Khan *describes a man who imagines paradise on Earth and tries to turn it into reality. But Coleridge said that even he wasn't sure what the poem really meant. According to him, he dreamt the lines during a nap!*

The Ant Explorer

Once a little sugar ant made up his mind to roam

To fare away far away, far away from home.

He had eaten all his breakfast, and he had his

 ma's consent

To see what he should chance to see and here's the

 way he went

Up and down a fern frond, round and round a stone,

Down a gloomy gully, where he loathed to be alone,

Up a mighty mountain range, seven inches high,

Through the fearful forest grass that nearly hid

 the sky,

Out along a bracken bridge, bending in the moss,

Till he reached a dreadful desert that was feet and feet

 across.

'Twas a dry, deserted desert, and a trackless

 land to tread;

He wished that he was home again and tucked up

 tight in bed.

His little legs were wobbly, his strength was

 nearly spent,

And so he turned around again and here's the way
   he went
Back along a bracken bridge, bending in the moss,
Through the fearful forest grass shutting out the sky,
Up a mighty mountain range, seven inches high,
Down a gloomy gully, where he loathed to be alone,
Up and down a fern frond, round and round a stone.
A dreary ant, a weary ant, resolved no more to roam,
He staggered up the garden path and popped
   back home.

Clarence James Dennis
1876–1938, b. Australia

Australian-born Clarence James Dennis was of Irish descent. He worked as a journalist and is best remembered as the author of a very successful book called The Songs of *a Sentimental Bloke, which was a love story about an ordinary man called Bill, his girl Doreen and his mate Ginger Mick, and was written in verse.*

The Joys of the Road

Now the joys of the road are chiefly these:

A crimson touch on the hard-wood trees;

A vagrant's morning wide and blue,

In early fall, when the wind walks too;

A shadowy highway cool and brown,

Alluring up and enticing down

From rippled water to dappled swamp,

From purple glory to scarlet pomp;

The outward eye, the quiet will,

And the striding heart from hill to hill;

The tempter apple over the fence;

The cobweb bloom on the yellow quince;

The palish asters along the wood,

A lyric touch of solitude;

An open hand, an easy shoe,

And a hope to make the day go through,

Another to sleep with, and a third

To wake me up at the voice of a bird;

A scrap of gossip at the ferry;

A comrade neither glum nor merry,

Who never defers and never demands,

But, smiling, takes the world in his hands,

Seeing it good as when God first saw

And gave it the weight of his will for law.

And oh, the joy that is never won,

But follows and follows the journeying sun,

By marsh and tide, by meadow and stream,

A will-o'-the-wind, a light-o'-dream,

The racy smell of the forest loam,

When the stealthy sad-heart leaves go home;

The broad gold wake of the afternoon;

The silent fleck of the cold new moon;

The sound of the hollow sea's release

From stormy tumult to starry peace;

With only another league to wend;

And two brown arms at the journey's end!

These are the joys of the open road

For him who travels without a load.

(William) Bliss Carman
1861–1929, b. Canada

William Bliss Carman was one of Canada's most highly rated poets of the 19th and 20th centuries. He was an editor and writer for literary journals and was well known for his anthology work, helping to compile the Oxford Book of American Verse (1927). Nature was a prominent feature in his poetry.

HOME AND WORK

❦

The everyday and familiar have been as much a source of inspiration as the extraordinary, a poet's sharp eye and senses sometimes making the banal brilliant, the commonplace breathtaking. Wordsworth catches the simple beauty of a city awakening in 'Upon Westminster Bridge', Oliver Goldsmith draws a kindly sketch of a dedicated teacher in 'The Village Schoolmaster', there is a caring and timeless parental moment in 'Hush, Little Baby', while in 'Ain't I a Woman', a black slave wonders at the injustice of her situation.

Upon Westminster Bridge

Earth has not anything to show more fair:
Dull would he be of soul who could pass by
A sight so touching in its majesty:
This City now doth like a garment wear

The beauty of the morning: silent, bare,
Ships, towers, domes, theatres, and temples lie
Open unto the fields, and to the sky,
All bright and glittering in the smokeless air.

Never did sun more beautifully steep
In his first splendour valley, rock, or hill;
Ne'er saw I, never felt, a calm so deep!

The river glideth at his own sweet will:
Dear God! the very houses seem asleep;
And all that mighty heart is lying still!

William Wordsworth
1770–1850, b. England

Wordsworth is perhaps the 'father of modern poetry', for he was the first poet to make his own feelings and thoughts the subject of his work. He and his best friend, Coleridge, were the first of several poets later grouped together as 'the Romantics'. Wordsworth wrote this poem while crossing Westminster Bridge on a coach to France. According to his notes, the city was transfigured in the dawn light with 'something like the purity of one of nature's own grand spectacles'.

I Hear America Singing

I hear America singing, the varied carols I hear,

Those of mechanics, each one singing his

as it should be blithe and strong,

The carpenter singing his

as he measures

his plank or beam,

The mason singing his

as he makes ready for work,

or leaves off work,

The boatman singing what

belongs to him in his boat,

the deckhand singing on the steamboat deck,

The shoemaker singing as he sits

on his bench, the hatter

singing as he stands,

The wood-cutter's song,

the ploughboy's on his way in the morning,

or at noon intermission or at sundown,

The delicious singing of the mother,

or of the young wife at work,

or of the girl sewing or washing,

Each singing what belongs to him

 or her and to none else,

The day what belongs to the day –

 at night the party of young fellows, robust, friendly,

Singing with open mouths their strong melodious songs.

Walt Whitman
1819–92, b. USA

Walt Whitman lived during the 'wild west' – the driving out of the Native Americans, the Gold Rush, the Civil War, the first trans-America railroad, and Custer's 'Last Stand'. Whitman had very little education and he was proud of being a 'working man' like the pioneers. He strove to write about ordinary people in ordinary language, and though he was determined to avoid being 'literary', his first book, Leaves of Grass (1855), is regarded as one of the greatest works of American literature.

A Description
of the Morning

Now hardly here and there an hackney-coach

Appearing, showed the ruddy morn's approach.

Now Betty from her Master's bed had flown,

And softly stole to discompose her own.

The slipshod 'Prentice from his Master's door,

Had pared the street, and sprinkled round the floor.

Now Moll had whirled her mop with dextrous airs,

Prepared to scrub the entry and the stairs.

The Youth with broomy stumps began to trace

The kennel edge, where wheels had worn the place.

The Smallcoal-man was heard with cadence deep,

Till drowned in shriller notes of Chimney-sweep.

Duns at his Lordship's gate began to meet;

And Brickdust Moll had

    screamed through half a street.

The Turnkey now his flock

    returning sees,

Duly let out a-nights to steal for fees.

The watchful Bailiffs take their

    silent stands;

And Schoolboys lag with satchels in

    their hands.

Jonathan Swift
1667–1745, b. Ireland

Jonathan Swift was born and educated in Ireland, but left due to political unrest and spent time in England working as a secretary to Sir William Temple. Temple had a vast library, which helped Swift develop intellectually, and it was during this time that he began writing. He is probably best known for his book Gulliver's Travels, but was also the author of many other fine works including the atmospheric poem 'A Description of the Morning'.

from Odyssey

Thus, near the gates conferring as they drew,
Argus, the dog, his ancient master knew;
He, not unconscious of the voice and tread,
Lifts to the sound his ear, and rears his head.
Bred by Ulysses, nourished at his board,
But ah, not fated long to please his lord!
To him, his swiftness and his strength were vain;
The voice of glory called him o'er the main.
Till then in every sylvan chase renowned,
With Argus, Argus, rung the woods around;
With him the youth pursued the goat or fawn,
Or traced the mazy leveret o'er the lawn.
Now left to man's ingratitude he lay,
Unhoused, neglected, in the public way,
And where on heaps the rich manure was spread,
Obscene with reptiles, took his sordid bed.

He knew his lord; he knew, and strove to meet,
In vain he strove to crawl, and kiss his feet;
Yet – all he could – his tail, his ears, his eyes
Salute his master, and confess his joys.

Soft pity touched the mighty master's soul;

Adown his cheek a tear unbidden stole,

Stole unperceived; he turned his head, and dried

The drop humane, then thus impassioned cried:

    'What noble beast in this abandoned state

Lies here all helpless at Ulysses' gate?

The dog, whom fate had granted to behold

His lord, when twenty tedious years had rolled,

Takes a last look, and having seen him, dies;

So closed for ever faithful Argus' eyes!

Homer

*circa 725–675*BC
translated by Alexander Pope
1688–1744, b. England

Odyssey, *like* Iliad, *is traditionally attributed to a mysterious poet called Homer, although it is now suspected that each poem had a different writer. Both epics draw from the saga of the Trojan War, but while* Iliad *focuses on the fighting,* Odyssey *tells of the warrior-king Odysseus's long and dangerous journey home. Alexander Pope wrote many widely acclaimed poems and essays of his own, but it was his Homeric translations that brought him fame and fortune.*

Ain't I a Woman?

That man over there say
   a woman needs to be helped into carriages
and lifted over ditches
   and to have the best place everywhere.
Nobody ever helped me into carriages
   or over mud puddles
     or gives me a best place ...

And ain't I a woman?

   Look at me

Look at my arm!

   I have plowed and planted

and gathered into barns

   and no man could head me …

And ain't I a woman?

   I could work as much

and eat as much as a man –

   when I could get to it –

and bear the lash as well

   and ain't I a woman?

I have borne thirteen children

   and seen most all sold into slavery

and when I cried out a mother's grief

   none but Jesus heard me …

And ain't I a woman?

    that little man in black there say

a woman can't have as much rights as a man

    cause Christ wasn't a woman

Where did your Christ come from?

    From God and a woman!

Man had nothing to do with him!

    If the first woman God ever made

was strong enough to turn the world

    upside down, all alone

together women ought to be able to turn it

    rightside up again.

Sojourner Truth

1797–1883, b. USA
adapted by Erlene Stetson

Sojourner Truth was born a black female slave when even white free women had few rights. She was freed by the New York Emancipation Act of 1827 and left New York in 1843 with only a bag of clothes and 25 cents. She spent the rest of her life campaigning for the rights of black people and women, and rose to become head councillor of Freedman's village in Virginia. This poem was originally a speech made at the Women's Rights Convention in Ohio, 1852.

Blacksmiths

Swarthy smoke-blackened smiths,
    smudged with soot,
Drive me to death with the din of
    their banging.
Men never knew such a noise at night!
Such clattering and clanging, such
    clamour of scoundrels!
Crabbed and crooked, they cry, 'Coal! Coal!'
And blow with their bellows till their brains burst.
'Huff! Puff!' pants one: 'Haff! Paff!' another.
They spit and they sprawl and they spin many yarns.
They grate and grind their teeth, and groan together,
Hot with the heaving of their hard hammers.
Aprons they have, of hide of the bull,
And greaves as leg-guards against glowing sparks.
Heavy hammers they have, and hit hard with them;
Sturdy strokes they strike on their steel anvils.

Lus, bus! Las, bas! they beat in turn –

Such a doleful sin, may the Devil destroy it!

The smith stretches a scrap, strikes a smaller,

Twines the two together, and tinkles a treble note:

Tik, tak! Hic, hac! Tiket, taket! Tyk, tak!

Bus, lus! Bas, las! Such a life they lead,

These Dobbin-dressers: Christ doom them

    to misery!

There's no rest at night for the noise of their

    water-fizzing.

Anonymous
circa 1425–50
translated from Medieval English by Brian Stone

This medieval poem is a highly accomplished example of the tradition of alliterative verse that existed in England before the Norman Conquest and enjoyed a revival at the time of Chaucer (circa 1343–1400). The style fits the subject perfectly – the clashing consonants brilliantly evoke the clanging of blacksmiths at work. However, the poem is unique for its shortness; other alliterative poems, such as Sir Gawain and the Green Knight, *are much longer.*

The Village Schoolmaster

Beside yon straggling fence that skirts the way
With blossom'd furze unprofitably gay,
There, in his mansion, skill'd to rule,
The village master taught his little school;
A man severe he was, and stern to view,
I knew him well, and every truant knew;
Well had the boding tremblers learn'd to trace
The day's disasters in his morning face;
Full well they laugh'd with counterfeited glee,
At all his jokes, for many a joke had he:
Full well the busy whisper, circling round,
Convey'd the dismal tidings when he frown'd:
Yet he was kind; or if severe in aught,
The love he bore to learning was in fault.
The village all declar'd how much he knew;
'Twas certain he could write, and cipher too:
Lands he could measure, terms and tides presage,
And e'en the story ran that he could gauge.
In arguing too, the person own'd his skill,

For e'en though vanquish'd he could argue still;

While words of learned length and thund'ring sound

Amazed the gazing rustics rang'd around;

And still they gaz'd and still the wonder grew,

That one small head could carry all he knew.

But past is all his fame. The very spot

Where many a time he triumph'd is forgot.

Oliver Goldsmith
1728–74, b. Ireland

Oliver Goldsmith was an inventive, wild genius who lived hard, played hard and worked hard. He worked as a hack writer turning out huge amounts of work on many subjects. He published histories of England, Rome and Greece, wrote biographies and the enduring play She Stoops to Conquer, *plus a famous novel* The Vicar of Wakefield. *The poem about the village schoolmaster is said to have been inspired by Goldsmith's own childhood teacher.*

Hush, Little Baby

Hush, little baby, don't say a word,

Papa's going to buy you a mocking bird.

If the mocking bird won't sing,

Papa's going to buy you a diamond ring.

If the diamond ring turns to brass,

Papa's going to buy you a looking-glass.

If the looking-glass get broke,

Papa's going to buy you a billy-goat.

If that billy-goat runs away,

Papa's going to buy you another today.

Anonymous

Throughout time parents have lulled their babies to sleep with gentle rhymes and songs. Lullabies have been passed down through the generations, they use simple language and metre, which give them their soporific effect.

From a Railway Carriage

Faster than fairies, faster than witches,
Bridges and houses, hedges and ditches;
And charging along like troops in a battle,
All through the meadows the horses and cattle:
All of the sights of the hill and the plain
Fly as thick as driving rain;
And ever again, in the wink of an eye,
Painted stations whistle by.

Here is a child who clambers and scrambles,
All by himself and gathering brambles;
Here is a tramp who stands and gazes;
And there is the green for stringing the daisies!
Here is a cart run away in the road
Lumping along with man and load;
And here is a mill, and there is a river:
Each a glimpse and gone for ever!

Robert Louis Stevenson
1850–94, b. Scotland

Robert Louis Stevenson is best known for his well-loved novels: the adventure stories **Treasure Island** (1883) and **Kidnapped** (1886), and **The Strange Case of Dr Jekyll and Mr Hyde** (1886). 'From a Railway Carriage' was published in his first volume of poetry, **A Child's Garden of Verses** (1885). Stevenson suffered from very poor health, and many of the poems in this book were written when he was lying ill in bed in Tahiti, remembering childhood holidays at his grandfather's home.

The Chimney Sweeper

When my mother died I was very young,

And my father sold me while yet my tongue

Could scarcely cry and 'weep! 'weep! 'weep! 'weep!'

So your chimneys I sweep, and in soot I sleep.

There's little Tom Dacre, who cried when his head,

That curl'd like a lamb's back, was shav'd: so I said

and 'Hush, Tom! never mind it, for when your

    head's bare

You know that the soot cannot spoil your white hair.'

And so he was quiet, and that very night,

As Tom was a-sleeping, he had such a sight!

That thousands of sweepers, Dick, Joe, Ned, and Jack,

Were all of them lock'd up in coffins of black.

And by came an Angel who had a bright key,

And he open'd the coffins and set them free;

Then down a green plain leaping, laughing, they run,

And wash in a river, and shine in the Sun.

Then naked and white, all their bags left behind,

They rise upon clouds and sport in the wind;

And the Angel told Tom, if he'd be a good boy,

He'd have God for his father, and never want joy.

And so Tom awoke; and we rose in the dark,

And got with our bags and our brushes to work,

Tho the morning was cold, Tom was happy and warm,

So if all do their duty they need not fear harm.

William Blake
1757–1827, b. England

The poem 'The Chimney Sweeper' appeared in William Blake's book of poems Songs of Innocence, which he published in 1789. Blake engraved the words and pictures onto copper plates and his wife Catherine coloured the plates. The book sold slowly in his lifetime and William Blake's hugely versatile talent and mind have only been recognized long after his death.

Old Thanksgiving Rhyme

The year has turned its circle,
The seasons come and go.
The harvest all is gathered in
And chilly north winds blow.

Orchards have shared their treasures,

The fields, their yellow grain,

So open wide the doorway –

Thanksgiving comes again!

Author unknown

*T*his American poem celebrates the time at the end of the harvest and the hard work done by all those working on the land. It is the onset of winter, the crops are safely gathered in and the cycle of seasons and work are about to start again.

Where's the Poker?

THE poker lost, poor Susan storm'd,
And all the rites of rage perform'd;
As scolding, crying, swearing, sweating,
Abusing, fidgeting, and fretting.
'Nothing but villany, and thieving;
Good heavens! what a world we live in!
If I don't find it in the morning,
I'll surely give my master warning.
He'd better far shut up his doors,
Than keep such good for nothing whores;
For wheresoe'er their trade they drive,
We vartuous bodies cannot thrive.'
Well may poor Susan grunt and groan;
Misfortunes never come alone,
But tread each other's heels in throngs,
For the next day she lost the tongs;
The salt box, colander, and pot
Soon shar'd the same untimely lot.
In vain she vails and wages spent
On new ones – for the new ones went.

There'd been (she swore) some dev'l or witch in,

To rob or plunder all the kitchen.

One night she to her chamber crept

(Where for a month she had not slept;

Her master being, to her seeming,

A better play fellow than dreaming).

Curse on the author of these wrongs,

In her own bed she found the tongs,

(Hang Thomas for an idle joker!)

In her own bed she found the poker,

With the salt box, pepper box, and kettle,

With all the culinary metal.

Be warn'd, ye fair, by Susan's crosses:

Keep chaste and guard yourselves from losses;

For if young girls delight in kissing,

No wonder that the poker's missing.

Christopher Smart
1722–71, b. England

The English poet Christopher Smart earned his living working in London writing for periodicals and composing songs for the popular theatre. He was a wild character and developed a religious mania, which led to him being confined to an asylum for a while. He produced admired works, one of which is the poem to his cat Jeoffry, an excerpt from Jubilate Agno.

The Lamplighter

My tea is nearly ready and the sun has left the sky.

It's time to take the window to see Leerie going by;

For every night at teatime and before you take

 your seat,

With lantern and with ladder he comes posting up

 the street.

Now Tom would be a driver and Maria go to sea,

And my papa's a banker and as rich as he can be;

But I, when I am stronger and can choose what I'm

to do,

O Leerie, I'll go round at night and light the lamps

with you!

For we are very lucky, with a lamp before the door,

And Leerie stops to light it as he lights so

many more;

And oh! before you hurry by with ladder and

with light;

O Leerie, see a little child and nod to him tonight!

Robert Louis Stevenson
1850–94, b. Scotland

Before the introduction of electricity, the lamplighter would go through the streets as dusk fell and light the gas lamps in the towns. In the morning, as day broke, he would extinguish the light and often call out to get the townsfolk out of bed. This poem of Robert Louis Stevenson evokes a time gone by and the child's voice is beautifully captured.

WAR AND HEROISM

Perhaps the best-known poem to characterize this section is 'The Charge of the Light Brigade', which captures in equal measure the valour and futility of war, but there are many other wars and many other acts of heroism immortalized by the poems here. Homer's lines from Iliad are possibly the most ancient, there are lines from the 8th-century Beowulf describing the heroic feats of the mythological prince, while two poems by Wilfred Owen from World War I graphically show that war has become a killing machine of industrial efficiency.

157

from The Charge of the Light Brigade

Half a league, half a league,
Half a league onward,
All in the valley of Death
Rode the six hundred.
'Forward, the Light Brigade!
Charge for the guns!' he said;
Into the valley of Death
Rode the six hundred.

'Forward, the Light Brigade!'
Was there a man dismay'd?
Not tho' the soldier knew
Someone had blunder'd:
Theirs not to make reply,
Theirs not to reason why,
Theirs but to do and die:
Into the valley of Death
Rode the six hundred.

Cannon to right of them,
Cannon to left of them,
Cannon in front of them
Volley'd and thunder'd;
Stormed at with shot and shell,
Boldly they rode and well,
Into the jaws of Death,
Into the mouth of Hell
Rode the six hundred.

Alfred, Lord Tennyson
1809–92, b. England

During the Crimean War, there was a charge on October 25, 1854 at Balaclava, where 247 out of 637 soldiers were killed or wounded – due to a misunderstood order. This poem appeared in the Examiner only weeks later. The line 'Someone had blunder'd', suggested by a phrase in a report in The Times, was omitted when it was published in 1855 in Maud, and Other Poems, but was later reinstated.

The Star-Spangled Banner

O say, can you see, by the dawn's early light,
    What so proudly we hailed at the twilight's last gleaming –
Whose broad stripes and bright stars, through the clouds of
    the fight,
O'er the ramparts we watched were so gallantly streaming!
    And the rocket's red glare, the bombs bursting in air,
Gave proof through the night that our flag was still there;
    O! say, does that star-spangled banner yet wave
O'er the land of the free, and the home of the brave?

On that shore dimly seen through the mists of the deep,
    Where the foe's haughty host in dread silence reposes,
What is that which the breeze, o'er the towering steep,
    As it fitfully flows, now conceals, now discloses?
Now it catches the gleam of the morning's first beam,
    In full glory reflected now shines on the stream;
Tis the star-spangled banner; O long may it wave
    O'er the land of the free, and the home of the brave!

And where is that band who so vauntingly swore

    That the havoc of war and the battles' confusion

A home and a country should leave us no more?

    Their blood has washed out their foul footsteps' pollution.

No refuge could save the hireling and slave

    From the terror of flight, or the gloom of the grave;

And the star-spangled banner in triumph doth wave

    O'er the land of the free, and the home of the brave.

O! thus be it ever, when freemen shall stand

    Between their loved homes and the war's desolation!

Blest with victory and peace, may the heav'n-rescued land

    Praise the power that hath made and preserved us a nation.

Then conquer we must, when our cause it is just,

And this be our motto – 'In God is our trust':

And the star-spangled banner in triumph shall wave

O'er the land of the free, and the home of the brave.

Francis Scott Key
1779–1843, b. USA

It was the sight of the American flag flying over Fort McHenry in Baltimore Harbour, during the 1812 war with Britain, that inspired lawyer and poet Francis Scott Key to write this poem. Written on the back of a letter, the poem is set to the tune of an English drinking song. It became the national anthem of the United States on March 3, 1931. A copy Key made of his original poem is in the Library of Congress.

Sir Patrick Spence

The king sits in Dumferling toune,
    Drinking the blude-reid wine:
'O whar will I get a guid sailor,
    To sail this schip of mine?'

Up and spak an eldern knicht,
    Sat at the king's richt kne:
'Sir Patrick Spence is the best sailor,
    That sails upon the se.'

The king has written a braid letter,
    And signed it wi' his hand;
And sent it to Sir Patrick Spence,
    Was walking on the sand.

The first line that Sir Patrick red,
    A loud lauch lauched he:
The next line that Sir Patrick red,
    The teir blinded his e'e.

O wha is this has don this deid,
    This ill deid don to me:
To send me out this time o' the yeir,
    To sail upon the se?

'Mak haste, mak haste, my mirry men all,
    Our guid schip sails the morne.'
'O say na sae, my master deir,
    For I feir a deadlie storme.

'Late, late yestreen I saw the new moone
    Wi' the auld moone in hir arme;
And I feir, I feir, my deir master,
    That we will com to harme.'

O our Scots nobles wer richt laith
    To weet their cork-heiled schoone;
Bot lang owre a' the play wer played,
    Thair hats they swam aboone.

O lang, lang may the ladies stand
    Wi' thair gold kems in their hair,
Waiting for thair ain deir lords,
    For they'll se thame na mair.

Haf owre, haf owre to Aberdour,
    It's fiftie fadom deip:
And thair lies guid Sir Patrick Spence,
    Wi' the Scots lords at his feit.

Anonymous

Thomas Percy (1729–1811), a grocer's son, was the first person to publish an English translation of a Chinese novel. This early Scottish ballad, full of tragedy and drama, was included in Percy's Reliques of Ancient English *Poetry (1765), a collection of historical songs, sonnets and romances. Percy took it from the most important source of our ballad literature, a manuscript written in mid-17th-century handwriting, which came to be known as the* Percy Folio.

from Iliad

Now shield with shield, with helmet helmet closed,
To armour armour, lance to lance opposed,
Host against host with shadowy squadrons drew,
The sounding darts in iron tempests flew,
Victors and vanquished joined promiscuous cries,
And shrilling shouts and dying groans arise;
With streaming blood the slippery fields are dyed,
And slaughtered heroes swell the dreadful tide.

As torrents roll, increased by numerous rills,
With rage impetuous down their echoing ills,
Rush to the vales, and poured along the plain,
Roar through a thousand channels to the main;
The distant shepherd trembling hears the sound:
So mix both hosts, and so their cries rebound.

Homer
circa 725–675BC
translated by Alexander Pope
1688–1744, b. England

*H*omer was more important to the Classical world than Shakespeare is to us today. His poems provided the basis of Ancient Greek and Roman education. Set in the imaginary heroic past of the Trojan War, Iliad *centres on the bitter quarrel between Agamemnon and Achilles, the greatest of the Greek warriors. Over 15,000 lines starkly describe the glory, and brutality, of war. This extract depicts the recommencing of battle between the two sides after a truce has been breached.*

Anthem for Doomed Youth

What passing-bells for these who die as cattle?
    Only the monstrous anger of the guns.
    Only the stuttering rifles' rapid rattle
Can patter out their hasty orisons.
No mockeries now for them; no prayers nor bells.
    Nor any voice of mourning save the choirs, –
The shrill, demented choirs of wailing shells;
    And bugles calling for them from sad shires.
What candles may be held to speed them all?
    Not in the hands of boys, but in their eyes
Shall shine the holy glimmers of goodbyes.
    The pallor of girls' brows shall be their pall;
Their flowers the tenderness of patient minds,
And each slow dusk a drawing down of blinds.

Wilfred Owen
1893–1918, b. England

*T*he son of a railway-worker,
Wilfred Owen read widely and
began writing poetry at an early age.
He taught English in Bordeaux in 1913,
and returned there in 1915 to join the
army. After enduring concussion and
trench-fever on the Somme, Owen was
sent to hospital in Edinburgh. There he
met Siegfried Sassoon (who was
suffering from shell-shock), who
encouraged him in his writing. Owen
returned to France in 1918 and won the
Military Cross, but was killed a week
before the Armistice.

from Beowulf

After these words the Weather-Geat prince
dived into the Mere – he did not care
to wait for an answer – and the waves closed over
the daring man. It was a day's space almost
before he could glimpse ground at the bottom.

The grim and greedy guardian of the flood,
keeping her hungry hundred-season watch,
discovered at once that one from above,
a human, had sounded the home of the monsters.
She felt for the man and fastened upon him
her terrible hooks; but no harm came thereby
to the hale body within – the harness so ringed him
that she could not drive her dire fingers
through the mesh of the mail-shirt masking his limbs.

When she came to the bottom she bore him to
    her lair,

the mere-wolf, pinioning the mail-clad prince.

Not all his courage could enable him

to draw his sword; but swarming through the water,

throngs of sea-beasts threw themselves upon him

with ripping tusks to tear his battle-coat,

tormenting monsters. Then the man found

that he was in some enemy hall

where there was no water to weigh upon him

and the power of the flood could not pluck
    him away,

sheltered by its roof: a shining light he saw,

a bright fire blazing clearly.

It was then that he saw the size of this water-hag,

damned thing of the deep. He dashed out his weapon,

not stinting the stroke, and with such strength and violence

that the circled sword screamed on her head

a strident battle-song. But the stranger saw

his battle-flame refuse to bite

or hurt her at all; the edge failed

its lord in his need. It had lived through many

hand-to-hand conflicts, and carved through the helmets

of fated men. This was the first time

that this rare treasure had betrayed its name.

Anonymous

circa 8th century
translated by Michael Alexander

Like the works of Homer, this Old English poem was originally performed aloud. Set in pagan 6th-century Scandinavia, it tells first how the hero Beowulf saves a hall of warriors from the monster Grendel. He then dives fearlessly into a lake to battle Grendel's mother in an underwater cave (as described in this extract). Finally, after 50 years as king, he dies defending his people by slaying a dragon. Beowulf and his exploits are paralleled in other Northern mythologies.

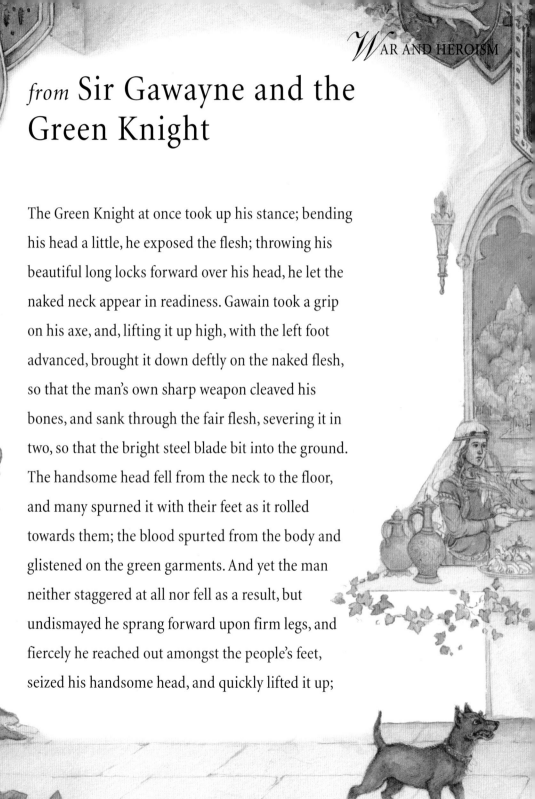

from Sir Gawayne and the Green Knight

The Green Knight at once took up his stance; bending his head a little, he exposed the flesh; throwing his beautiful long locks forward over his head, he let the naked neck appear in readiness. Gawain took a grip on his axe, and, lifting it up high, with the left foot advanced, brought it down deftly on the naked flesh, so that the man's own sharp weapon cleaved his bones, and sank through the fair flesh, severing it in two, so that the bright steel blade bit into the ground. The handsome head fell from the neck to the floor, and many spurned it with their feet as it rolled towards them; the blood spurted from the body and glistened on the green garments. And yet the man neither staggered at all nor fell as a result, but undismayed he sprang forward upon firm legs, and fiercely he reached out amongst the people's feet, seized his handsome head, and quickly lifted it up;

and then, turning to his horse, caught the bridle,
stepped into the stirrup and vaulted up,
holding his head by the hair in his hand, and the
knight seated himself in his saddle as calmly as if he
had suffered no mishap, though he sat there headless
now. He twisted his trunk around, that gruesome
bleeding corpse; many were afraid of him by the time
he had had his say.

For he actually held up the head in his hand, turning
the face toward the greatest nobles on the dais,
and it lifted up its eyelids and stared wide-eyed, and
its mouth spoke, as you may now hear, to this effect:
'See to it, Gawain, that you are ready to go as you
promised, and search until you find me, sir, as
faithfully as you have sworn in this hall, in the
hearing of these knights. Make your way to the Green
Chapel, I charge you, to receive such a knock as you
have given – you have well deserved to be promptly
repaid on New Year's morning. Many men know me,
the Knight of the Green Chapel; and so, if you seek to
find me, you will not fail. Come, therefore, or you are

bound to be called a coward.' With a violent jerk he pulled the reins round and, his head in his hand, dashed out at the door of the hall, so that the sparks flew from the stones at his horse's hooves. To what land he went none there knew, any more than they knew where he had come from …

Anonymous

circa 1375
translated by W R J Barron

*T*his famous medieval poem combines English 'green man' folklore with Arthurian legend. A huge green warrior bursts into King Arthur's New Year Feast. He challenges a knight to cut off his head – on condition that he can return the blow in a year's time. Sir

Gawain courageously accepts, but is horrified to find that the Green Knight simply picks up his head and rides away, laughing. Twelve months later, brave Gawain has to set off to honour the bargain …

Drummer Hodge

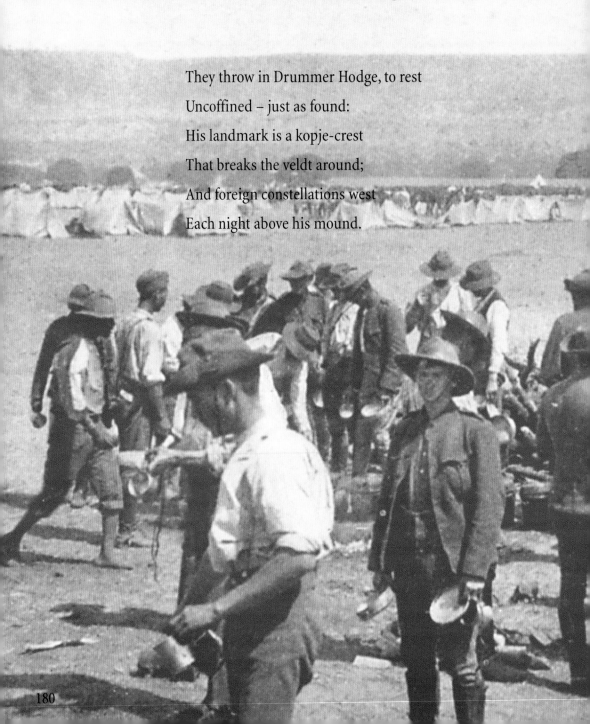

They throw in Drummer Hodge, to rest

Uncoffined – just as found:

His landmark is a kopje-crest

That breaks the veldt around;

And foreign constellations west

Each night above his mound.

Young Hodge the Drummer never knew –

Fresh from his Wessex home –

The meaning of the broad Karoo,

The Bush, the dusty loam,

And why uprose to nightly view

Strange stars amid the gloam.

Yet portion of that unknown plain

Will Hodge forever be;

His homely Northern breast and brain

Grow to some Southern tree,

And strange-eyed constellation reign

His stars eternally.

Thomas Hardy
1840–1928, b. England

*T**homas Hardy wrote poems about the Boer War and World War I. 'Drummer Hodge' is the story of the death of a young Englishman, who* *fought in South Africa in the Boer War. The Boer War lasted from 1899 until 1902 with huge losses of men far away from their homeland.*

from Morte d'Arthur

So all day long the noise of battle rolled

Among the mountains by the winter sea;

Until King Arthur's table, man by man,

Had fallen in Lyonnesse about their Lord,

King Arthur. Then, because his wound was deep,

The bold Sir Bedivere uplifted him,

Sir Bedivere, the last of all his knights,

And bore him to a chapel nigh the field,

A broken chancel with a broken cross,

That stood on a dark strait of barren land.

On one side lay the Ocean, and on one

Lay a great water, and the moon was full.

Then spake King Arthur to Sir Bedivere:

'…I perish by this people which I made, –

Though Merlin sware that I should come again

To rule once more – but let what will be, be,

I am so deeply smitten through the helm

That without help I cannot last till morn.

Thou therefore take my brand Excalibur,

Which was my pride: for thou rememberest how

In those old days, one summer noon, an arm

Rose up from out the bosom of the lake,

Clothed in white samite, mystic, wonderful,

Holding the sword – and how I rowed across

And took it, and have worn it, like a king:

And, wheresoever I am sung or told

In aftertime, this also shall be known:

But now delay not: take Excalibur,
And fling him far into the middle mere:
Watch what thou seest, and lightly bring
me word.'
… Then quickly rose Sir Bedivere, and ran,
And, leaping down the ridges lightly, plunged
Among the bulrush-beds, and clutched the sword,
And strongly wheeled and threw it. The great brand

Made lightnings in the splendour of the moon,

And flashing round and round, and whirled in an arch,

Shot like a streamer of the northern morn,

Seen where the moving isles of winter shock

By night, with noises of the northern sea.

So flashed and fell the brand Excalibur:

But ere he dipt the surface, rose an arm

Clothed in white samite, mystic, wonderful,

And caught him by the hilt, and brandished him

Three times, and drew him under in the mere.

Alfred, Lord Tennyson
1809–92, b. England

Tennyson began this poem in 1833, soon after the death of his best friend, Arthur Hallam. As a source, he used Malory's huge collection of Arthurian legends 'Le Morte d'Arthur' (finished 1470). The poem tells of the king's last moments, after battling the usurping Mordred. In 1869, Tennyson added 169 lines to the start and 29 lines at the end, and incorporated the poem into his 12-book cycle of Arthurian ballads, 'Idylls of the King'.

Dulce et Decorum Est

Bent double, like old beggars under sacks,
Knock-kneed, coughing like hags, we cursed through
  sludge,
Till on the haunting flares we turned our backs
And towards our distant rest began to trudge.
Men marched asleep. Many had lost their boots
But limped on, blood-shod. All went lame; all blind;
Drunk with fatigue; deaf even to the hoots
Of tired, outstripped Five-Nines that dropped behind.
Gas! Gas! Quick, boys! – An ecstasy of fumbling,
Fitting the clumsy helmets just in time;
But someone still was yelling out and stumbling
And flound'ring like a man in fire or lime . . .
Dim, through the misty panes and thick green light,
As under a green sea, I saw him drowning.

In all my dreams, before my helpless sight,
He plunges at me, guttering, choking, drowning.

If in some smothering dreams you too could pace

Behind the wagon that we flung him in,

And watch the white eyes writhing in his face,

His hanging face, like a devil's sick of sin;

If you could hear, at every jolt, the blood

Come gargling from the froth-corrupted lungs,

Obscene as cancer, bitter as the cud

Of vile, incurable sores on innocent tongues, –

My friend, you would not tell with such high zest

To children ardent for some desperate glory,

The old Lie: Dulce et decorum est

Pro patria mori.

Wilfred Owen
1893–1918, b. England

Owen is now considered to be the foremost poet of World War I. However, only five of his poems were published during his lifetime and they achieved no success – like Siegfried Sassoon's war poetry. The public were captivated by Rupert Brooke, whose poems speak of glory, heroism and love. The work of both Sassoon and Owen tells bleakly of the miserable reality of the trenches and expresses contempt for war.

ANIMALS

A whole menagerie parades before you in this delightful section, praising everything from the well-organized bee to the watchful vixen. A flea becomes a symbol of love-making in Donne's poem, Thomas Gray wittily mourns his drowned pet cat in his ode, Walt Whitman describes the majesty of two eagles' courtship display and Edward Lear crews his pea-green boat with two charming animal characters in his ever-amusing 'The Owl and the Pussy-Cat'.

For so Work the Honey-bees

For so work the honey-bees,

Creatures that by a rule in nature teach

The act of order to a peopled kingdom.

They have a king and officers of sorts;

Where some, like magistrates, correct at home,

Others, like merchants, venture trade abroad,

Others, like soldiers, armèd in their stings,

Make boot upon the summer's velvet buds;

Which pillage they with merry march bring home

To the tent-royal of their emperor.

William Shakespeare
1564–1616, b. England

*T*he quotation from William Shakespeare's play Henry V about the honey-bees draws parallels with human behaviour and society. The play was first performed at The Globe theatre in London in 1599. It completes the saga of the Lancaster Rebellion, the Hundred Years' War and the Wars of the Roses in a series of plays covering events in English history between 1398 and 1485.

Ode on the Death of a Favourite Cat

'Twas on a lofty vase's side,
Where China's gayest art had dyed
The azure flowers, that blow;
Demurest of the tabby kind,
The pensive Selima reclined,
Gazed on the lake below

Her conscious tail her joy declared;
The fair round face, the snowy beard,
The velvet of her paws,
Her coat that with the tortoise vies,
Her ears of jet and emerald eyes,
She saw; and purred applause.

Still had she gazed; but 'midst the tide
Two angel forms were seen to glide,
The Genii of the stream:
Their scaly armour's Tyrian hue

Through richest purple to the view
Betrayed a golden gleam.

The hapless nymph with wonder saw:
A whisker first and then a claw,
With many an ardent wish,
She stretched in vain to reach the prize.
What female heart can gold despise?
What cat's averse to fish?

Presumptuous maid! with looks intent
Again she stretched, again she bent,
Nor knew the gulf between.
(Malignant Fate sat by and smiled)
The slipp'ry verge her feet beguiled,
She tumbled headlong in.
Eight times emerging from the flood
She mewed to every watery god,

Some speedy aid to send.

No dolphin came, no Nereid stirred:

Nor cruel Tom nor Susan heard.

A favourite has no friend!

From hence, ye beauties, undeceived,

Know, one false step is ne'er retrieved,

And be with caution bold.

Not all that tempts your wandering eyes

And heedless hearts is lawful prize;

Nor all that glisters gold.

Thomas Gray
1716–71, b. England

The English poet Thomas Gray was a shy character who shunned publicity and declined the Poet Laureateship. His output of poetry was small but includes the famous 'Elegy Written in a Country Churchyard', which is one of the most celebrated poems of its century. His light-hearted poem about the drowning of a cat trying to hook out a goldfish from a pond was written in memory of the death of his friend Herbert Walpole's cat Selima.

Ladybird, Ladybird

Ladybird, ladybird, fly away home,

Your house in on fire and your children are gone,

All except one and that's little Ann,

For she crept under the frying pan.

Traditional rhyme

Ladybirds are seen in gardens in Britain in the warm summer months and are most commonly red with black spots. This rhyme is traditionally chanted when one of these pretty little insects lands on a person.

The Cow

The friendly cow all red and white,

I love with all my heart:

She gives me cream with all her might,

To eat with apple-tart.

She wanders lowing here and there,

And yet she cannot stray,

All in the pleasant open air,

The pleasant light of day;

And blown by all the winds that pass

And wet with all the showers,

She walks among the meadow grass

And eats the meadow flowers.

Robert Louis Stevenson
1850–94, b. Scotland

Robert Louis Stevenson was raised mainly by his nanny Alison Cunningham and he dedicated his A Child's Garden of Verses *to her. His sweet poem about the cow was included in the collection. Stevenson was ill* throughout his childhood and spent much time in bed reading and writing. Later he was to travel mainly for his health and write a number of exciting novels, including Treasure Island.

The Dalliance of the Eagles

Skirting the river road, (my forenoon walk, my rest,)

Skyward in air a sudden muffled sound, the dalliance of the eagles,

The rushing amorous contact high in space together,

The clinching interlocking claws, a living, fierce, gyrating wheel,

Four beating wings, two beaks, a swirling mass tight grappling,

In tumbling turning clustering loops, straight downward falling.

Till o'er the river pois'd, the twain yet one, a moment's lull,

A motionless still balance in the air, then parting, talons loosing,

Upward again on slow-firm pinions slanting, their separate
　　diverse flight,

She hers, he his, pursuing.

Walt Whitman
1819–92, b. USA

The vividly descriptive 'The Dalliance of the Eagles' was written in 1880 and is included in Walt Whitman's famous work Leaves of Grass. *The first edition was self-published and Whitman helped the printers set the type. Whitman's style was highly innovative and influential and he is one of the greatest American poets.*

The Horses of the Sea

The horses of the sea
Rear a foaming crest,
But the horses of the land
Serve us the best.
The horses of the land
Munch corn and clover,
While the foaming sea-horses
Toss and turn over.

Christina Rossetti
1830–94, b. England

When Fishes Set Umbrellas Up

When fishes set umbrellas up

If the rain-drops run,

Lizards will want their parasols

To shade them from the sun.

Christina Rossetti

1830–94, b. England

Christina Rossetti was closely associated with the Pre-Raphaelite movement which counted Dante Gabriel Rossetti, her brother, as one of its founding members. This group was dedicated to painting serious subjects, embracing nature and shunning styles after Raphael. Their subjects were often biblical and literary. Christina was a profoundly religious woman who wrote devotional prose and poetry, children's verses and poems with love, nature and fantasy themes. She was the first Pre-Raphaelite to enjoy literary success.

Upon a Snail

She goes but softly, but she goeth sure,

She stumbles not, as stronger creatures do.

Her journey's shorter, so she may endure

Better than they which do much farther go.

She makes no noise, but stilly seizeth on

The flower or herb appointed for her food,

The which she quietly doth feed upon

While others range and glare, but find no good.

And though she doth but very softly go,

However, 'tis not fast nor slow, but sure;

And certainly they that do travel so,

The prize they do aim at they do procure.

John Bunyan
1628–88, b. England

After supporting the side of Parliament in the English Civil War, John Bunyan changed his life, embraced religion and became a travelling preacher. He spent a long period of time in gaol during which he wrote many books with religious themes. John Bunyan's most famous work is the allegorical novel **The Pilgrim's Progress.**

from The Flea

Mark but this flea, and mark in this,

How little that which thou deniest me is;

It suck'd me first, and now sucks thee,

And in this flea our two bloods mingled be.

Thou know'st that this cannot be said

A sin, nor shame, nor loss of maidenhead;

Yet this enjoys before it woo,

And pamper'd swells with one blood made of two;

And this, alas! is more than we would do.

John Donne
1572–1631, b. England

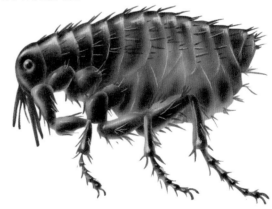

John Donne was a one of a group of 17th-century poets known as the Metaphysical poets. Marvell, Vaughan and Traherne were also in the group. Their poetry was witty and inventive using irony and wordplay. In 'The Flea', Donne uses the flea as an erotic image.

The Twa Corbies

As I was walking all alane,
I heard twa corbies making a mane;
The tane unto the t'other say,
'Where sall we gang and dine to-day,
Where sall we gang and dine to-day?'

'In behint yon auld fail dyke,
I wot there lies a new slain knight;
And naebody kens that he lies there,
But his hawk, his honnd, and lady fair,
His hawk, his honnd, and lady fair.

'His hound is to the hunting gane,
His hawk to fetch the wild-fowl hame,
His lady 'a ta'en another mate,
So we may mak our dinner sweet,
We may mak our dinner sweet.

'Ye'll sit on his white hause-bane,

And I'll pike out his bonny blue een;

Wi ae lock o his gowden hair

We'll theek our nest when it grows bare,

We'll theek our nest when it grows bare.'

'Mony a one for him makes mane,

But nane sall ken where he is gane;

Oer his white banes, when they are bare,

The wind sail blaw for evennair,

The wind sail blaw for evennair.'

Author unknown

Written in Scottish dialect 'The Twa Corbies' dates back to the 17th century. Corbies are ravens or crows. The story is grim, telling of the two birds in a conversation about picking over the body of a fallen knight. It creates a sinister atmosphere with a macabre ending.

Frog

Ancient silent pond

Then a frog jumped right in!

Watersound: kerplunk

Matsuo Basho
circa 1644–94, b. Japan
translated by John S Major

Heron

The lightning flashes
And slashing through
the darkness,
A night-heron's screech.

Matsuo Basho
circa 1644–94, b. Japan

A haiku is a form of Japanese poetry, which dates from the 16th century. Its subjects are traditionally drawn from nature and the words must consist of 17 syllables exactly, which are arranged in three lines: of five syllables, then seven syllables, then five syllables. The poet Basho is one of the great masters of this poetic form and this famous frog haiku has been widely imitated by western writers.

from The Lamb

Little Lamb, who made thee

Does thou know who made thee

Gave thee life and bid thee feed.

By the stream and o'er the mead;

Gave thee clothing of delight,

Softest clothing woolly bright;

Gave thee such a tender voice.

Making all the vales rejoice:

Little Lamb who made thee

Does thou know who made thee

Little Lamb I'll tell thee,

Little Lamb I'll tell thee;

He is called by thy name,

For he calls himself a Lamb:

He is meek & he is mild,

He became a little child

I a child & thou a lamb,

We are called by His name,

Little Lamb God bless thee,

Little Lamb God bless thee.

William Blake
1757–1827, b. England

William Blake recorded that in his earlier years he had experienced visions of angels and had conversations with the Angel Gabriel, the Virgin Mary and other biblical figures. He was regarded as an eccentric in his lifetime and somewhat of a rebel. William Blake's creative output included engravings, poems and paintings, which are much admired today.

The Owl and the Pussy-Cat

The Owl and the Pussy-cat went to sea

    In a beautiful pea-green boat,

They took some honey, and plenty of money,

    Wrapped up in a five-pound note.

The Owl looked up to the stars above,

    And sang to a small guitar,

'O lovely Pussy! O Pussy, my love,

    What a beautiful Pussy you are,

        You are,

        You are!

    What a beautiful Pussy you are!'

Pussy said to the Owl, 'You elegant fowl!

    How charmingly sweet you sing!

O let us be married! too long have we tarried:

    But what shall we do for a ring?'

They sailed away, for a year and a day,

    To the land where the Bong-tree grows

And there in a wood a Piggy-wig stood

    With a ring at the end of his nose,

      His nose,

      His nose,

    With a ring at the end of his nose.

'Dear Pig, are you willing to sell for one shilling

    Your ring?' Said the Piggy, 'I will.'

So they took it away, and were married next day

    By the Turkey who lives on the hill.

They dined on mince, and slices of quince,

    Which they ate with a runcible spoon;

And hand in hand, on the edge of the sand,

    They danced by the light of the moon,

        The moon,

        The moon,

    They danced by the light of the moon.

Edward Lear
1812–88, b. England

Edward Lear spent his early working life as a draughtsman for the Zoological Society and then as an artist for the British Museum. His close study of animal life is often echoed in his much-loved limericks and nonsense verses. He travelled widely in his lifetime and produced many fine paintings as well as poetry.

Duck's Ditty

All along the backwater,
Through the rushes tall,
Ducks are a-dabbling.
Up tails all!

Ducks' tails, drakes' tails,
Yellow feet a-quiver,
Yellow bills all out of sight
Busy in the river!

Slushy green undergrowth

Where the roach swim

Here we keep our larder,

Cool and full and dim.

Every one for what he likes!

We like to be

Head down, tails up,

Dabbling free!

High in the blue above

Swifts whirl and call

We are down a-dabbling

Up tails all!

Kenneth Grahame
1859–1932, b. Scotland

*K*enneth Grahame was born in Edinburgh but spent some of his childhood with his maternal grandmother, who lived in a house with a large garden by the River Thames. This setting was the backdrop of his most famous book The Wind in the Willows (1908), which established his reputation as a writer of children's books. The characters of Ratty, Mole and Toad have been favourites of children over the generations and were originally created for Kenneth Grahame's son Alistair, who was known to his family as Mouse.

Lizard

A lizard ran out on a rock and looked up, listening
no doubt to the sounding of the spheres.
And what a dandy fellow! the right toss of a chin for you
and swirl of a tail!

If men were as much men as lizards are lizards
they'd be worth looking at.

D H Lawrence
1885–1930, b. England

*D*avid Herbert Lawrence began *writing in his youth and went on to become a controversial figure in the world of literature. He suffered from bronchitis all his life and travelled to* warm climates such as Ceylon, Australia and Mexico. His famous novels include Women in Love, Lady Chatterley's Lover and Sons and Lovers.

The Maldive Shark

About the Shark, phlegmatical one,

Pale sot of the Maldive sea,

The sleek little pilot-fish, azure and slim,

How alert in attendance be.

From his saw-pit of mouth, from his charnel of maw,

They have nothing of harm to dread,

But liquidly glide on his ghastly flank

Or before his Gorgonian head;

Or lurk in the port of serrated teeth

In white triple tiers of glittering gates,

And there find a haven when peril's abroad,

An asylum in jaws of the Fates!

They are friends; and friendly they guide him to prey,

Yet never partake of the treat —

Eyes and brains to the dotard lethargic and dull,

Pale ravener of horrible meat.

Herman Melville
1819–91, b. USA

Herman Melville was a cabin boy on a whaler. He later joined the US Navy, beginning a series of voyages on ships sailing both the South Seas and the Atlantic. He was best known for his novels about the sea and especially for his masterpiece Moby Dick, which was published in 1851.

To a Butterfly

Stay near me – do not take thy flight!

A little longer stay in sight!

Much converse do I find in thee,

Historian of my infancy!

Float near me; do not yet depart!

Dead times revive in thee:

Thou bring'st, gay creature as thou art!

A solemn image to my heart,

My father's family!

Oh! pleasant, pleasant were the days,

The time, when, in our childish plays,

My sister Emmeline and I

Together chased the butterfly!

A very hunter did I rush

Upon the prey:- with leaps and springs

I followed on from brake to bush;

But she, God love her, feared to brush

The dust from off its wings.

William Wordsworth
1770–1850, b. England

William Wordsworth was one of the Lake poets, a group of English poets who lived in the Lake District in the north-west of England. The other Lake poets were Samuel Taylor Coleridge and Robert Southey.

All three were also part of the Romantic movement of the late 1700s and early 1800s. They were all influenced by the beautiful landscape around them and its rich natural history.

The Vixen

Among the taller wood with ivy hung,

The old fox plays and dances round her young.

She snuffs and barks if any passes by

And swings her tail and turns prepared to fly,

The horseman hurries by, she bolts to see,

And turns agen, from danger never free.

If any stands she runs among the poles

And barks and snaps and drives them in the holes.

The shepherd sees them and the boy goes by

And gets a stick and progs the hole to try.

They get all still and lie in safety sure,

And out again when everything's secure,

And start and snap at blackbirds bouncing by

To fight and catch the great white butterfly.

John Clare
1793–1864, b. England

John Clare was born into a poor, rural family in Northamptonshire in 1793. He was herding animals at the age of seven. He had virtually no schooling and started verse-writing after studying James Thompson's Seasons. Clare's poems were wonderfully descriptive of the English countryside in the 19th century. Initially Clare's verses were well received. Clare made friends with the poet Charles Lamb and other literary figures who helped support him financially when the fashion changed and his style of poetry was no longer so popular.

Pied Beauty

Glory be to God for dappled things,

For skies of couple-colour as a brinded cow,

For rose-moles all in stipple upon trout that swim;

Fresh-firecoal chestnut-falls, finches' wings;

Landscape plotted and pieced, fold, fallow

    and plough,

And all trades, their gear and tackle and trim.

All things counter, original, spare, strange,

Whatever is fickle, freckled (who knows how?)

With swift, slow; sweet, sour; adazzle, dim.

He fathers-forth whose beauty is past change;

Praise him.

Gerard Manley Hopkins
1844–89, b. England

The poems of Gerard Manley Hopkins, the English Jesuit priest, are much admired today. He was a Victorian poet, virtually unknown in his lifetime, whose poetry was very modern in style. Whilst a student at Oxford University he struck up a friendship with the poet Robert Bridges, and it was Bridges who collected and published Hopkins' poems in 1918.

The Dragonfly

Today I saw the dragonfly
Come from the wells where he did lie.

An inner impulse rent the veil
Of his old husk: from head to tail
Came out clear plates of sapphire mail.

He dried his wings: like gauze they grew;
Thro' crofts and pastures wet with dew
A living flash of light he flew.

Alfred, Lord Tennyson
1809–1892, b. England

*T*he poet Alfred, Lord Tennyson showed great talent as a writer from an early age. He went on to become one of the foremost Victorian poets. He was the author of many works including 'The Lotus-Eaters', 'The Charge of the Light Brigade' and 'In Memoriam'. Tennyson succeeded William Wordsworth as Poet Laureate in 1850.

The Cat and the Fiddle

Hey-diddle-diddle,

The cat and the fiddle,

The cow jumped over the moon;

The little dog laughed to see such fun,

And the dish ran away with the spoon.

Traditional rhyme

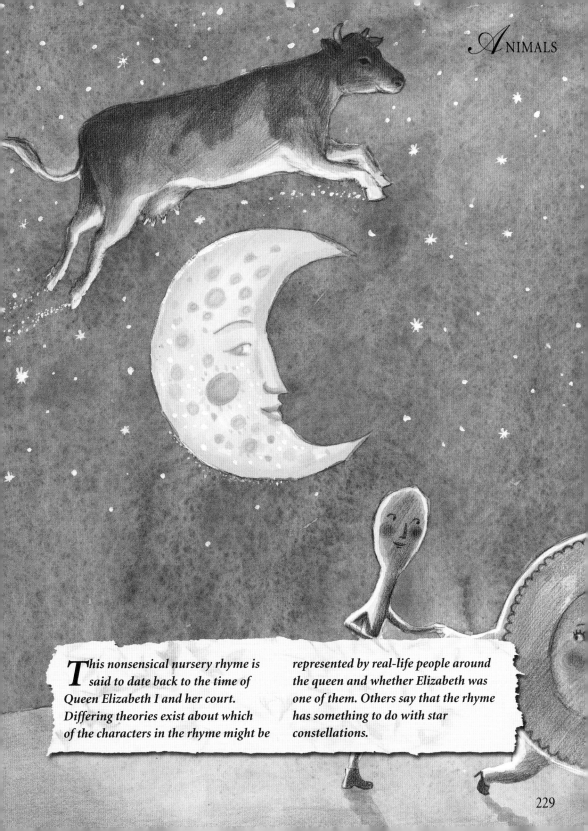

This nonsensical nursery rhyme is said to date back to the time of Queen Elizabeth I and her court. Differing theories exist about which of the characters in the rhyme might be represented by real-life people around the queen and whether Elizabeth was one of them. Others say that the rhyme has something to do with star constellations.

CHILDREN'S POEMS

The poems we first read or hear are usually written for children. They can have memorable sounds and visions that stay with us for a lifetime. This section may well evoke memories of childhood or be a good start for introducing children to the pleasures of poetry and nursery rhymes. Many will be familiar with names such as Robert Louis Stephenson, Henry Wadsworth Longfellow and Charles and Mary Lamb, but here also are delightful poems by lesser-known poets such as Mary Howitt, Julia Fletcher Carney and George MacDonald.

A Guinea Pig

There was a little guinea pig,
Who being little, was not big;
He always walked upon his feet,
And never fasted when he eat.

When from a place he run away,
He never at the place did stay;
And while he run, as I am told,
He never stood still for young or old.

He often squeaked, and sometimes violent,

And when he squeaked he never was silent.

Though never instructed by a cat,

He knew a mouse was not a rat.

One day, as I am certified,

He took a whim, and fairly died;

And as I am told by men of sense,

He never has been living since.

Anonymous

circa 1775

The guinea pig is now a popular pet and was introduced into Europe in the 16th century by Dutch explorers. It is related to the chinchilla and the porcupine and originates from the Andes Mountains in South America. Guinea pigs were probably first domesticated by the Indians from Peru who used them for sacrificial offerings to their gods, and for food.

Buttercups and Daisies

Buttercups and daisies –
Oh the pretty flowers,
Coming ere the springtime
To tell of sunny hours.
While the trees are leafless,
While the fields are bare,
Buttercups and daisies
Spring up here and there.

Ere the snowdrop peepeth,
Ere the crocus bold,
Ere the early primrose
Opes its paly gold,
Somewhere on a sunny bank
Buttercups are bright;
Somewhere 'mong the frozen grass
Peeps the daisy white.

Little hardy flowers
Like to children poor,
Playing in their sturdy health
By their mother's door:
Purple with the north wind,
Yet alert and bold;
Fearing not and caring not,
Though they be a-cold.

What to them is weather!
What are stormy showers!
Buttercups and daisies
Are these human flowers!
He who gave them hardship
And a life of care,
Gave them likewise hardy strength,
And patient hearts, to bear.

Welcome yellow buttercups,

Welcome daisies white,

Ye are in my spirit

Visioned, a delight!

Coming ere the springtime

Of sunny hours to tell –

Speaking to our hearts of Him

Who doeth all things well.

Mary Howitt
1799–1888, b.England

The English poet Mary Howitt had a great love of nature. She came from a Quaker background. Her husband William also took up writing and they travelled widely. Mary Howitt was good at languages and translated the stories of Hans Christian Andersen. She was associated with many other famous writers of the day such as Mrs Gaskell, Charles Dickens, William Wordsworth and Alfred, Lord Tennyson.

There Was an Old Man

There was an Old Man with a beard,

Who said, 'It is just as I feared!–

Two owls and a hen,

Four larks and a wren,

Have all built their nests in my beard!'

Edward Lear
1812–88, b. England

Edward Lear published his first Book of Nonsense in 1846. He composed and illustrated all 72 limericks, but as was customary with children's books, his work was published anonymously. In the third edition, published in 1861, his name did appear and it contained 112 limericks. Limericks are five lines long and a popular form of humorous and often nonsensical verse. Lear much preferred the term 'nonsense'.

Two Little Kittens

Two little kittens, one stormy night,
Began to quarrel, and then to fight;
One had a mouse, the other had none,
And that's the way the quarrel begun.

'I'll have that mouse,' said the biggest cat;
'You'll have that mouse? We'll see about that!'
'I will have that mouse,' said the eldest son;
'You shan't have the mouse,' said the little one.

I told you before 'twas a stormy night
When these two little kittens began to fight;
The old woman seized her sweeping broom,
And swept the two kittens right out of the room.

The ground was covered with frost and snow,
And the two little kittens had nowhere to go;
So they laid them down on the mat at the door,
While the old woman finished sweeping the floor.

Then they crept in, as quiet as mice,

All wet with the snow, and cold as ice,

For they found it was better, that stormy night,

To lie down and sleep than to quarrel and fight.

Anonymous

It is thought that this poem was written around 1880. A good imagination and keen observation of how kittens play, fight and get tired out has been woven into a charming poem known by children over several generations.

Where Did You Come from, Baby Dear?

Where did you come from, baby dear?
Out of the everywhere into here.

Where did you get your eyes so blue?
Out of the sky as I came through.

What makes the light in them sparkle and spin?
Some of the starry spikes left in.

Where did you get that little tear?
I found it waiting when I got here.

What makes your forehead so smooth and high?
A soft hand stroked it as I went by.

What makes your cheek like a warm white rose?
I saw something better than anyone knows.

Whence that three-cornered smile of bliss?
Three angels gave me at once a kiss.

Where did you get this pearly ear?
God spoke, and it came out to hear.

Where did you get those arms and hands?
Love made itself into hooks and bands.

Feet, whence did you come, you darling things?
From the same box as the cherubs' wings.

How did they all just come to be you?
God thought about me, and so I grew.

But how did you come to us, you dear?
God thought about you, and so I am here.

George MacDonald
1824–1905, b. Scotland

George MacDonald was a Scottish novelist, clergyman and poet. He published over 50 volumes of fiction, children's stories, sermons and verse. His real success came with his novels of Scottish country life and he met notable authors such as Ruskin, Tennyson and Carlyle. George MacDonald made many friends, including Emerson on a lecture tour in the United States. In his poetry there is a pervading spiritual quality and the poem 'Where Did You Come from, Baby Dear?' illustrates this very well.

My Shadow

I have a little shadow that goes in and out with me,
And what can be the use of him is more than I can see.
He is very, very like me from the heels
　　up to the head;
And I see him jump before me, when I jump
　　into my bed.

The funniest things about him is the
　　way he likes to grow –
Not at all like proper children,
　　which is always very slow;
For he sometimes shoots up taller like an
　　India rubber ball,
And he sometimes gets so little that there's none of him
　　at all.
He hasn't got a notion of how children ought to play,

And can only make a fool of me in every sort of way.

He stays so close beside me, he's a coward

    you can see;

I'd think shame to stick to nursie as that

    shadow sticks to me!

One morning, very early, before the sun was up,

I rose and found the shining dew on every buttercup;

But my lazy little shadow, like an arrant sleepy-head,

Had stayed at home behind me and was fast

    asleep in bed.

Robert Louis Stevenson
1850–94, b. Scotland

This delightful poem about a child's shadow going everywhere with him, changing size in different lights, has a sweet, innocent quality. Robert Louis Stevenson was a keen observer of life and when he travelled was always jotting down his observations in little pocket books. He was a highly regarded and popular writer at the end of the 19th century and regained that reputation in the mid-20th century.

Little Things

Little drops of water,
Little grains of sand,
Make the mighty ocean
And the beauteous land.

And the little moments,
Humble though they be,
Make the mighty ages
Of eternity.

So our little errors
Lead the soul away,
From the paths of virtue
Into sin to stray.

Little deeds of kindness,
Little words of love,
Make our earth an Eden,
Like the heaven above.

Julia Fletcher Carney
1824–1908, b. USA

*I*n 1845 Bostonian schoolteacher Julia
Fletcher Carney wrote a poem for a
class of schoolchildren doing bible
studies. She wanted to emphasize the
value of small things and wrote her
poem 'Little Things'. The poem was
later published in **McGuffey's Reader.**

This was a series of textbooks, seen by
most schools in the United States, which
sought to instil a sense of morality in the
reader and contained religious
messages. Julia Fletcher Carney's poem
became known throughout the world.

The Fieldmouse

Where the acorn tumbles down,
Where the ash tree sheds its berry,
With your fur so soft and brown,
With your eye so round and merry,
Scarcely moving the long grass,
Fieldmouse, I can see you pass.

Little thing, in what dark den,
Lie you all the winter sleeping?
Till warm weather comes again,
Then once more I see you peeping
Round about the tall tree roots,
Nibbling at their fallen fruits.

Fieldmouse, fieldmouse, do not go,
Where the farmer stacks his treasure,
Find the nut that falls below,
Eat the acorn at your pleasure,
But you must not steal the grain
He has stacked with so much pain.

Make your hole where mosses spring,

Underneath the tall oak's shadow,

Pretty, quiet harmless thing,

Play about the sunny meadow.

Keep away from corn and house,

None will harm you, little mouse.

Cecil Frances Alexander
1818–95, b. Ireland

The famous hymn-writer Cecil Frances Alexander was born in County Wicklow, Ireland in 1818. She began writing poetry at the age of nine. She published Verses for Holy Seasons *in 1846 which was followed by* Hymns for Little Children *in 1849 and this contained some of her best-loved works such as* 'Once in Royal David's City' *and* 'There Is a Green Hill Far Away'.

There Was a Little Girl

There was a little girl

Who had a little curl

Right in the middle of the forehead.

When she was good

She was very, very good,

But when she was bad she was horrid.

Henry Wadsworth Longfellow

1807–82, b. USA

Henry Wadsworth Longfellow was the most popular American poet of the 19th century and published his first poem at the age of 13. It is said that he had his second daughter in his arms, and as he walked her up and down he composed the charming poem about the little girl with the curl.

The First Tooth

Through the house what busy joy,

Just because the infant boy

Has a tiny tooth to show!

I have got a double row,

All as white, and all as small;

Yet no one cares for mine at all.

He can say but half a word,

Yet that single sound's preferred

To all the words that I can say

In the longest summer day.

He cannot walk, yet if he put

With mimic motion out his foot,

As if he thought he were advancing,

It's prized more than my best dancing.

Charles and Mary Lamb
1775–1834 and 1764–1847, b. England

Charles and Mary Lamb both suffered from periods of insanity and Mary was kept in an asylum after murdering their mother. She was eventually released into the care of her brother. The pair collaborated and produced Tales from Shakespeare *and various poems. Charles Lamb was part of a group of young writers including Shelley, Hazlitt and Leigh Hunt and had a lifelong friendship with Samuel Taylor Coleridge.*

The Father's Vineyard

As round their dying father's bed
His sons attend, the peasant said:
'Children, deep hid from prying eyes,
A treasure in my vineyard lies;
When you have laid me in the grave,
Dig, search – and your reward you'll have.'

'Father,' cries one, 'but where's the spot?'
He sighs! he sinks! he answers not.

The tedious burial service over,
Home go his sons, and straight explore
Each corner of the vineyard round,
Dig up, beat, break, and sift the ground;
Yet though to search so well inclined,
Nor gold, nor treasure could they find;
But when the autumn next drew near,
A double vintage crowned the year.

'Now,' quoth the peasant's wisest son,

'Our father's legacy is know,

In yon rich purple grapes 'tis seen,

Which, but for digging, never had been.

Then let us all reflect with pleasure.

That labour is the source of treasure.'

Anonymous

Here is a moral tale. The poem is anonymous and could have been written at any time. It is easy to imagine the sons at their father's bedside hanging on his every wise word and taking his promise of treasure literally. Their inheritance is a fine yield of grapes and the knowledge of how to manage the vineyard in the future.

Doctor Foster

Doctor Foster went to Gloucester

In a shower of rain;

He stepped in a puddle,

Right up to his middle,

And never went there again.

Author unknown

*T*his old nonsense rhyme is usually prompted by heavy rainfall, and is often heard in the playground. It is reputed to be based on the English king, Edward I, riding to Gloucester and falling from his horse into a muddy puddle.

You Are Old,
Father William

'You are old, Father William,' the young man said,

'And your hair has become very white;

And yet you incessantly stand on your head –

Do you think, at your age, it is right?'

~

'In my youth,' Father William replied to his son,

'I feared it might injure the brain;

But, now that I'm perfectly sure I have none,

Why, I do it again and again.'

~

'You are old,' said the youth, 'as I mentioned before,

And have grown most uncommonly fat;

Yet you turned a back somersault in at the door –

Pray, what is the reason of that?'

'In my youth,' said the sage, as he shook his grey locks,

'I kept all my limbs very supple

By the use of this ointment – one shilling the box –

Allow me to sell you a couple?'

~

'You are old,' said the youth, 'and your jaws are too weak

For anything tougher than suet;

Yet you finished the goose, with the bones and the back –

Pray, how did you manage to do it?'

~

'In my youth,' said his father, 'I took to the law,

And argued each case with my wife;

And the muscular strength, which it gave to my jaw,

Has lasted the rest of my life.'

'You are old,' said the youth, 'one would hardly suppose

That your eye was steady as ever;

Yet, you balanced an eel on the end of your nose-

What made you so awfully clever?'

~

'I have answered three questions, and that is enough,'

Said his father. 'Don't give yourself airs!

Do you think I can listen all day to such stuff?

Be off, or I'll kick you downstairs!'

Lewis Carroll
1832–98, b. England

Lewis Carroll considered himself to be a man of science who also happened to write nonsense. The poem about Father William appears in Alice's Adventures in Wonderland, *which was* published in 1865. The book was a collection of stories Lewis Carroll told to the young Alice Liddell, daughter of one of his Oxford friends.

Where Go the Boats?

Dark brown is the river,
Golden is the sand.
It flows along for ever,
With trees on either hand.

Green leaves a-floating,
Castles of the foam,
Boats of mine a-boating –
Where will all come home?

On goes the river,

And out past the mill,

Away down the valley,

Away down the hill.

Away down the river,

A hundred miles or more,

Other little children

Shall bring my boats ashore.

Robert Louis Stevenson
1850–94, b. Scotland

Robert Louis Stevenson revelled in travel, he loved the sea, boats and adventure. He spent time in a variety of ships sailing to exotic places such as Tahiti, Tonga, Australia and Samoa.

This poem gives a sense of the pleasure of wandering through new landscapes and the satisfaction of seeing new places and distant lands.

Upon the Swallow

This pretty bird, oh, how she flies and sings!

But could she do so if she had not wings?

Her wings bespeak my faith, her songs my peace;

When I believe and sing, my doubtings cease.

Robert Herrick

1591–1674, b. England

*L*ondon-born Robert Herrick was a cleric and poet. He studied at Cambridge University and was later ordained as an Episcopal minister. King Charles I granted him a living in Devon, where he wrote some of his best work. Other notable poets writing at the same time were Andrew Marvell, George Herbert and John Donne.

Robin Redbreast

Goodbye, goodbye to Summer!

For Summer's nearly done;

The garden smiling faintly,

Cool breezes in the sun;

Our Thrushes now are silent,

Our Swallows flown away –

But Robin's here, in coat of brown,

With ruddy breast-knot gay.

Robin, Robin Redbreast,

O Robin dear!

Robin singing sweetly

In the falling of the year.

Bright yellow, red, and orange,

The leaves come down in hosts;

The trees are Indian Princes,

But soon they'll turn to Ghosts;

The leathery pears and apples

Hang russet on the bough,

It's Autumn, Autumn, Autumn late,

'Twill soon be winter now.

Robin, Robin Redbreast,

O Robin dear!

And what will this poor Robin do?

For pinching days are near.

The fireside for the Cricket,

The wheatsack for the Mouse,

When trembling night-winds whistle

And moan all round the house;

The frosty ways like iron,

The branches plumed with snow –

Alas! in Winter, dead, and dark,

Where can poor Robin go?

Robin, Robin Redbreast,

O Robin dear!

And a crumb of bread for Robin,

His little heart to cheer.

William Allingham
1824–89, b. Ireland

William Allingham was born in Donegal. He was a civil servant who had literary connections. He wrote for Leigh Hunt's London Journal and was part of the Rossetti circle. Many of his poems were sold in Ireland as halfpenny sheets. He also wrote the poem that starts 'Up the airy mountain, down the rushy glen' called 'The Fairies'. The poem about Robin Redbreast is a lovely evocation of the oncoming winter months.

The Old Woman Who Lived in a Shoe

There was an old woman

who lived in a shoe,

She had so many children

she didn't know what to do.

She gave them some broth

without any bread;

She whipped them all soundly

and put them to bed.

Traditional rhyme

The nursery rhyme 'The Old Women Who Lived in a Shoe' is very old. A version of it first appeared in print in 1797. Its origin might date from the ancient custom of throwing a shoe after the bride when she left for her honeymoon. This was a blessing on the newly wed couple and the hope for a family in the future.

Ride a Cock-Horse

Ride a cock-horse to Banbury Cross,

To see a fine lady upon a white horse;

Rings on her fingers and bells on her toes,

She shall have music wherever she goes.

Traditional rhyme

This famous old nursery rhyme is said to relate to a visit from Queen Elizabeth I to the Oxfordshire town of Banbury. Riding a large stallion, the cock-horse, the queen wore rings on her fingers and bells at the end of her pointed-toed shoes. She was visiting the town to see the newly erected stone cross and the townsfolk decorated the streets and provided minstrels to make 'music wherever she goes'.

As I Was Going to St Ives

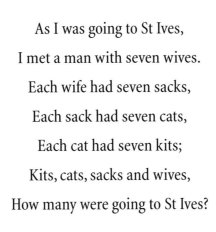

As I was going to St Ives,

I met a man with seven wives.

Each wife had seven sacks,

Each sack had seven cats,

Each cat had seven kits;

Kits, cats, sacks and wives,

How many were going to St Ives?

Traditional rhyme

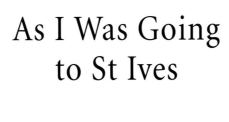

The humorous verse about the man going to St Ives poses a trick question to the reader. He met a lot of people and cats coming the other way!

It is used to improve logic and deductive skills. The rhyme can be traced back in published form to 1730.

WIT AND HUMOUR

---

*The fact that poetry can make us laugh
(if only quietly within) reveals what a wonderfully
versatile medium it is. From tongue twisters such
as 'Fleet Flight' and Lewis Carroll's own flights of
fancy, to the nonsense poems of Edward Lear,
T W Connor's music hall lyrics and the charming
anonymous rhymes that have appeared
spontaneously through the centuries, there
is a funny side to this section that is
cheery and frivolous.*

Fleet Flight

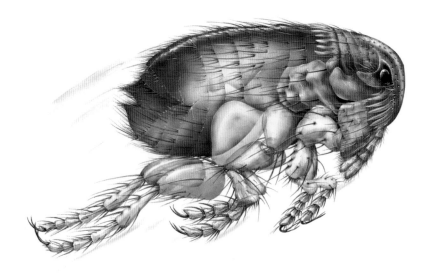

A flea met a fly in a flue,

Said the flea let us fly

Said the fly let us flee

so they flew through a flaw in the flue.

Anonymous

This poem has no known author but its humour travels well over time. The flea is not everyone's favourite creature but it is used to make a very funny, tongue-twisting verse with lots of wordplay.

As I Was Climbing up the Stair

As I was climbing up the stair
I met a man who wasn't there;
He wasn't there again to-day:
Oh, how I wish he'd go away!

Anonymous

*T*he poem 'As I Was Climbing up the Stair' is an anonymous verse, which makes one smile at its complete silliness. This nonsense verse conforms to the norm by following a rhyme scheme, embracing the absurd and being very funny.

Lizzie Borden

Lizzie Borden took an axe

And gave her mother forty whacks

When she saw what she had done

She gave her father forty-one.

Author unknown

A gruesome double-murder took place in Fall River, Massachusetts in 1892. In the following year Lizzie Borden stood trial in one of America's most famous and controversial trials, which was closely followed by the public.

Lizzie Borden was the daughter of the murdered couple and was eventually found not guilty of the crime. This macabre verse was composed at the time.

A Toadstool Comes up

A toadstool comes up in a night,

Learn the lesson, little folk –

An oak grows on a hundred years,

But then it is an oak.

Christina Rossetti
1830–94, b. England

*I*n 1872 a collection called **Sing-Song** written by Christina Rossetti was released. The poems are partly a remembrance of her own happy, early childhood. She was in her early forties when they were published. Although she had no children of her own she delighted in her siblings' families. 'Sing-Song' was dedicated to James Bagot Cayley's nephew. Christina had loved Cayley but rejected his proposal of marriage because they had differing thoughts on religion.

I Always Eat My Peas with Honey

I always eat my peas with honey;

I've done it all my life.

They do taste kind of funny

but it keeps them on my knife.

Anonymous

*T*here is something so silly about this poem but its logic seems sound. Peas must taste very strange with honey but it could be the perfect answer to an age-old problem of how to keep one's peas on the knife; except that in polite circles it is considered proper to use a fork! There is no authorship given for the poem but it is widely known.

The Lobster Quadrille

'Will you walk a little faster?' said a whiting to a snail,
'There's a porpoise close behind us, and he's treading
    on my tail.
See how eagerly the lobsters and the turtles all
    advance!
They are waiting on the shingle – will you come and
    join the dance?

Will you, won't you, will you, won't you, will you join
 the dance?
Will you, won't you, will you, won't you, won't you join
 the dance?

'You can really have no notion how delightful it will be
When they take us up and throw us, with the lobsters,
 out to sea!'
But the snail replied 'Too far, too far!' and gave a look
 askance –
Said he thanked the whiting kindly, but he would not
 join the dance.
Would not, could not, would not, could not, would not
 join the dance.
Would not, could not, would not, could not, could not
 join the dance.

'What matters it how far we go?' his scaly friend replied.

'There is another shore, you know, upon the other side.

The further off from England the nearer is to France,

Then turn not pale, beloved snail, but come and join the dance.

Will you, won't you, will you, won't you, will you join the dance?'

Lewis Carroll
1832–98, b. England

This poem appears in Chapter 10 of Lewis Carroll's book Alice in Wonderland. *It was written in 1865 during the Victorian era, a time of propriety and strict morals, but Carroll recognized how to combine his sense of the absurd with a story popular with both children and adults.*

If You Should Meet a Crocodile

If you should meet a Crocodile

Don't take a stick and poke him;

Ignore the welcome in his smile,

Be careful not to stroke him.

For as he sleeps upon the Nile,

He thinner gets and thinner;

And whene'er you meet a Crocodile

He's ready for his dinner.

Anonymous

There is an air of impending danger with the crocodile lurking on the riverbank waiting for his dinner.

The author of this poem is unknown but had a malevolent sense of humour.

The Budding Bronx

De spring is sprung

Der grass is riz

I wonder where dem boidies is?

Der little boids is on der wing.

Ain't dat absoid?

Der little wings is on der boid!

Anonymous

Thirty Purple Birds

Toity poiple boids

Sitt'n on der coib

A-choipin' and a-boipin

An' eat'n doity worms.

Anonymous

When reading these nonsense verses you can hear the true accent of New York. The city is made up of five boroughs separated by different waterways. Brooklyn and Queens occupy the west portion of Long Island. Staten Island and Manhattan are on their own land mass and the Bronx is to the north and remains attached to the New York State mainland. Over the centuries immigrants from all over the world have settled in New York giving it a richly diverse and unique atmosphere.

from The Jumblies

They went to sea in a Sieve, they did,

In a Sieve they went to sea;

In spite of all their friends could say,

On a winter's morn, on a stormy day,

In a Sieve they went to sea!

And when the Sieve turned round and round,

And everyone cried, 'You'll all be drowned!'

They called aloud, 'Our Sieve ain't big,

But we don't care a button, we don't care a fig!

In a Sieve we'll go to sea.'

Far and few, far and few,

Are the lands where the Jumblies live;

Their heads are green, and their hands are blue,

And they went to sea in a Sieve.

Edward Lear
1812–88, b. England

Artist Edward Lear suffered from epilepsy, depression and loneliness, and was at his happiest when amusing children with his 'nonsenses'. His first Book of Nonsense (1846) was inspired by the Earl of Derby's grandchildren, whom he met while drawing the Earl's animals. Other volumes of comic verse include Botany and Alphabets (1871), from which come 'The Owl and the Pussy-Cat' and 'The Jumblies'.

The Cantaloupe

Side by side in the crowded streets,
    Amid its ebb and flow,
We walked together one autumn morn;
    ('Twas many years ago!)
The markets blushed with fruits and flowers;
    (Both Memory and Hope!)
You stopped and bought me at the stall,
    A spicy cantaloupe.
We drained together its honeyed wine,
    We cast the seeds away;
I slipped and fell on the moony rinds,
    And you took me home in a dray!
The honeyed wine of your love is drained;
    I limp from the fall I had;
The snow-flakes muffle the empty stall,
    And everything is sad.

The sky is an inkstand, upside down,
    It splashes the world with gloom;
The earth is full of skeleton bones,
    And the sea is a wobbling tomb!

Bayard Taylor
1825–78, b. USA

Bayard Taylor was a poet-wanderer and chronicled his journeys at home and abroad. He was a newspaper correspondent, novelist and poet and from an early age had wanted to see more of the world. The poem 'The Cantaloupe' is a mixture of love and humour.

The Little Turtle

There was a little turtle.

He lived in a box.

He swam in a puddle

He climbed on the rocks

He snapped at a mosquito.

He snapped at a flea.

He snapped at a minnow.

And he snapped at me.

He caught the mosquito.

He caught the flea.

He caught the minnow.

But he didn't catch me.

Vachel Lindsay

1879–1931, b. USA

Vachel Lindsay was born in Springfield, Illinois, birthplace of Abraham Lincoln. Lindsay spent much of his life walking across the country, distributing copies of his poems, and giving live performances in exchange for his bed and board. He was known for his flamboyant style of delivering his poetry. Vachel Lindsay took his own life in 1931.

She Was a Sweet Little Dicky Bird

It was at the Pantomime that Mabel and I did meet,

She was in the ballet, front row, and I in a five shilling
seat.

She was dressed like a dicky bird, beautiful wings she
had on,

With a figure divine –

I wished she were mine –

On her I was totally gone.

She was a sweet little dicky bird.

Tweet-tweet-tweet! she went.

Sweetly she sang to me

Till all my money was spent.

Then she went off song.

We parted on fighting terms.

She was one of the early birds,

And I was one of the worms.

T W Connor
dates unknown

T W Connor wrote a large number of songs in the early part of the 20th century, which were performed in the music halls. The verse about the dear little dicky bird is a great favourite from the time of live shows, where the audience joined in singing along with the artists on stage. Although strictly a song, it is often quoted as a poem. It was written in 1895.

Mountains of Mourne

Oh, Mary, this London's a wonderful sight,

Wid the people here workin' by day and by night:

They don't sow potatoes, nor barley, nor wheat,

But there's gangs o' them diggin' for gold in the

    street –

At least, when I axed them, that's what I was told,

So I just took a hand at this diggin' for gold,

But for all that I found there, I might as well be

Where the Mountains o' Mourne sweep down to

    the sea.

I believe that, when writin', a wish you expressed

As to how the fine ladies in London were dressed.

Well, if you'll believe me, when axed to a ball,

They don't wear a top to their dresses at all!

Oh, I've seen them meself, and you could not, in thrath,

Say if they were bound for a ball or a bath –

Don't be startin' them fashions now, Mary Machree

Where the Mountains o' Mourne sweep down to the sea.

I seen England's King from the top of a 'bus –

I never knew him, though he means to know us:

And though by the Saxon we once were oppressed,

Still, I cheered – God forgive me – I cheered wid the rest

And now that he's visited Erin's green shore,

We'll be much better friends than we've been heretofore,

When we've got all we want, we're as quiet as can be

Where the Mountains o' Mourne sweep down to the sea.

You remember young Peter O'Loughlin, of course –

Well, here he is now at the head o' the Force.

I met him to-day, I was crossin' the Strand,

And he stopped the whole street wid wan wave of
    his hand –

And there we stood talking of days that are gone,

While the whole population of London looked on;

But for all these great powers, he's wishful like me,

To be back where dark Mourne sweeps down to
    the sea.

There's beautiful girls here - oh, never mind!

With beautiful shapes Nature never designed,

And lovely complexions, all roses and crame,

But O'Loughlin remarked wid regard to them same:

'That if at those roses you venture to sip,

The colour might all come away on your lip,'

So I'll wait for the wild rose that's waitin' for me—

Where the Mountains o' Mourne sweep down to

    the sea.

William Percy French
1854–1920, b. Ireland

William Percy French studied engineering at Trinity College, Dublin, but spent a lot of his time playing the banjo, composing songs and painting watercolours. After his wife's untimely death he toured the country on his bicycle painting pictures and developed a one-man show performing the songs he had composed.

I Intended an Ode

I intended an Ode,

…And it turn'd to a Sonnet

It began à la mode,

I intended an Ode;

But Rose cross'd the road

…In her latest new bonnet;

I intended an Ode;

…And it turn'd to a Sonnet.

Henry Austin Dobson
1840–1924, b. England

Henry Austin Dobson was a poet and essayist and worked as a civil servant. He had a great love and knowledge of the 18th century and wrote biographies of Henry Fielding, Oliver Goldsmith and Fanny Burney, among others.

The Pig

It was an evening in November

As I very well remember,

I was strolling down the street in drunken pride,

But my knees were all a-flutter,

And I landed in the gutter

And a pig came up and lay down by my side.

Yes, I lay there in the gutter

Thinking thoughts I could not utter,

When a colleen passing by did softly say

'You can tell a man who boozes

By the company he chooses' –

And the pig got up and slowly walked away.

Anonymous

One wonders if the anonymous verses about the man who had too much to drink and found himself spurned by a pig, taught him any kind of lesson! There is a very gentle pace about this funny poem and its unexpected last line.

Topsy-Turvy World

If the butterfly courted the bee,

And the owl the porcupine;

If the churches were built in the sea,

And three times one was nine;

If the pony rode his master,

If the buttercups ate the cows,

If the cat had the dire disaster

To be worried, sir, by the mouse;

If mamma, sir, sold the baby

To a gypsy for half-a-crown;

If a gentleman, sir, was a lady –

The world would be Upside Down!

If any or all of these wonders

Should ever come about,

I should not consider them blunders,

For I should be Inside Out!

Albert Midlane
1825–1909, b. Isle of Wight

Albert Midlane said that his Sunday school teacher inspired him to write poetry. Midlane became a businessman but throughout his life wrote over 300 hymns. 'Topsy-Turvy World' has a sense of celebration and a dash of nonsense.

For Want of a Nail

For want of a nail the shoe was lost,

For want of a shoe the horse was lost,

For want of a horse the rider was lost,

For want of a rider the battle was lost,

For want of a battle the kingdom was lost,

And all for the want of a horseshoe nail.

Traditional rhyme

*T*his witty old nursery rhyme has a chastising note about it, explaining the consequences following a thoughtless act. Because of the references to horses, battles, kingdoms and riders, it is thought to have originated in England.

INTO THE SHADOWS

——∞——

Some memorable thoughts from some great poets take us into the darkest corners in this section. It begins with the despairing contemplations of a prisoner and the dramatic horror of a shipwreck. There are glimpses of other worldly creatures and monsters from the ocean depths. Then come dark and painful musings before stark visions of hell itself.

from The Ballad of Reading Gaol

There is no chapel on the day
On which they hang a man:
The Chaplain's heart is far too sick,
Or his face is far too wan,
Or there is that written in his eyes
Which none should look upon.

So they kept us close till nigh on noon,
And then they rang the bell,
And the Warders with their jingling keys
Opened each listening cell,
And down the iron stair we tramped,
Each from his separate Hell.

Out into God's sweet air we went,

But not in wonted way,

For this man's face was white with fear,

And that man's face was grey,

And I never saw sad men who looked

So wistfully at the day.

I never saw sad men who looked

With such a wistful eye

Upon that little tent of blue

We prisoners call the sky,

And at every careless cloud that passed

In happy freedom by.

The Warders strutted up and down,
And kept their herd of brutes,
Their uniforms were spick and span,
And they wore their Sunday suits,
But we knew the work they had been at,
By the quicklime on their boots.

For where a grave had opened wide,
There was no grave at all:
Only a stretch of mud and sand
By the hideous prison-wall,
And a little heaping of burning lime,
That the man should have his pall.

For three long years they will not sow
Or root or seedling there:
For three long years the unblessed spot
Will sterile be and bare,
And look upon the wondering sky
With unreproachful stare.

They think a murderer's heart would taint
Each simple seed they sow.
It is not true! God's kindly earth
Is kindlier than men know,
And the red rose would but blow more red,
The white rose whiter blow.

Oscar Wilde
1854–1900, b. Ireland

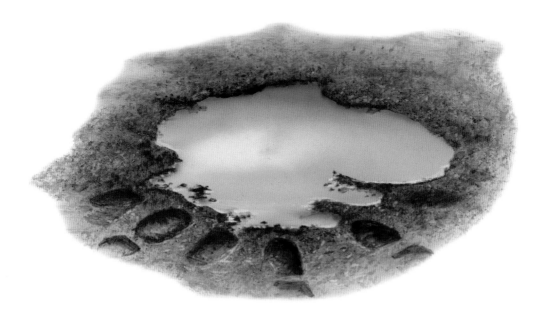

*O*scar Wilde was imprisoned in Reading Gaol between 1895 and 1897 for homosexual offences. He wrote 'The Ballad of Reading Gaol' in France a year after his release. A flamboyant personality and brilliant wit, Wilde is most famous for the volume of fairy stories **The Happy Prince and Other Tales** *(1888), written for his sons, his only novel* **The Picture of Dorian Gray** *(1890), which caused scandal, and the play* **The Importance of Being Earnest** *(1895).*

from The Wreck of the Deutschland

On Saturday sailed from Bremen,

American-outward-bound,

Take settler and seamen, tell men with women,

Two hundred souls in the round –

O Father, not under thy feathers nor ever as guessing

The goal was a shoal, of a fourth the doom to be drowned;

Yet did the dark side of the bay of thy blessing

Not vault them, the million of rounds of thy mercy not

   reeve even them in?

Into the snows she sweeps,

Hurling the haven behind,

The Deutschland, on Sunday; and so the sky keeps,

For the infinite air is unkind,

And the sea flint-flake, black-backed in the regular blow,

Sitting Eastnortheast, in cursed quarter, the wind;

Wiry and white-fiery and whirlwind-swivellèd snow

Spins to the widow-making unchilding unfathering deeps.

She drove in the dark to leeward,

She struck – not a reef or a rock

But the combs of a smother of sand: night drew her

Dead to the Kentish Knock;

And she beat the bank down with her bows and the ride of

   her keel;

The breakers rolled on her beam with ruinous shock;

And canvas and compass, the whorl and the wheel

Idle for ever to waft her or wind her with, these she endured.

Hope had grown grey hairs,

Hope had mourning on,

Trenched with tears, carved with cares,

Hope was twelve hours gone;

And frightful a nightfall folded rueful a day

Nor rescue, only rocket and lightship, shone,

And lives at last were washing away:

To the shrouds they took, – they shook in the hurling and

   horrible airs.

One stirred from the rigging to save

The wild woman-kind below,

With a rope's end round the man, handy and brave –

He was pitched to his death at a blow,

For all his dreadnought breast and braids of thew:

They could tell him for hours, dandled the to and fro

Through the cobbled foam-fleece. What could he do

With the burl of the fountains of air, buck and the flood of

   the wave?

They fought with God's cold –

And they could not and fell to the deck

(Crushed them) or water (and drowned them) or rolled

With the sea-romp over the wreck,

Night roared, with the heart-break hearing a heart-broke rabble,

The woman's wailing, the crying of child without check –

Till a lionness arose breasting the babble,

A prophetess towered in the tumult, a virginal tongue told.

Gerard Manley Hopkins
1844–89, b. England

Only Hopkins' closest friends knew during his lifetime that he was a poet. Now he is famous for his bold and creative use of language and rhythm. This poem was inspired by the loss of **The Deutschland** *in December 1875.*

Hopkins grapples with the question of how God can allow tragedy and human suffering, and finds the answer in Christ's own pain and sacrifice – success is often through 'failure'.

from The Fairies

Up the airy mountain

Down the rushy glen,

We daren't go a-hunting

For fear of little men;

Wee folk, good folk,

Trooping all together;

Green jacket, red cap,

And white owl's feather!

William Allingham
1824–89, b. Ireland

Customs Officer William Allingham composed several collections and anthologies of verse for children, some with illustrations by Rossetti, Millais, Kate Greenaway, and his wife, Helen Paterson. 'The Fairies' (written in 1840) was published in his Poems (1850). It is based on a traditional song that was adapted in Scotland to the Jacobite cause: 'Tis up the rocky mountain and down the mossy glen, We darena gang a milking for Charlie and his men…'

Jabberwocky

Twas brillig, and the slithy toves

Did gyre and gimble in the wabe;

All mimsy were the borogoves,

And the mome raths outgrabe.

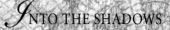

'Beware the Jabberwock, my son!

The jaws that bite, the claws that catch!

Beware the Jubjub bird, and shun

The frumious Bandersnatch!'

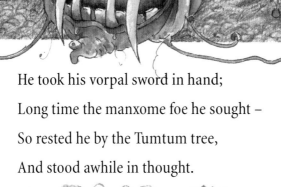

He took his vorpal sword in hand;

Long time the manxome foe he sought –

So rested he by the Tumtum tree,

And stood awhile in thought.

And, as in uffish thought he stood,

The Jabberwock, with eyes of flame,

Came whiffling through the tulgey wood,

And burbled as it came!

One, two! One two! And through and through

The vorpal blade went snicker-snack!

He left it dead, and with its head

He went galumphing back.

'And hast thou slain the Jabberwock?
Come to my arms, my beamish boy!
O frabjous day! Callooh! Callay!'
He chortled in his joy.

'Twas brillig, and the slithy toves
Did gyre and gimble in the wabe:
All mimsy were the borogoves,
And the mome raths outgrabe.

Lewis Carroll
1832–98, b. England

*Lewis Carroll was the pen-name of
Charles Lutwidge Dodgson. While
a maths lecturer at Christ Church,
Oxford, he wrote the classic novels
Alice's Adventures in Wonderland
(1865) and Through the Looking-Glass
and What Alice Found There (1871).*

*His poetry includes Phantasmagoria
and Other Poems (1869) and The
Hunting of the Snark (1876). Most
writing for children at the time had a
moral message, and Carroll's fantastical
novels and comic verse were immensely
popular.*

from The Pied Piper of Hamelin

Into the street the Piper stept,
  Smiling first a little smile,
As if he knew what magic slept
  In his quiet pipe the while;
Then, like a musical adept,
To blow the pipe his lips he wrinkled,
And green and blue his sharp eyes twinkled,
Like a candle-flame where salt is sprinkled;

And ere three shrill notes the pipe uttered,

You heard as if an army muttered;

And the muttering grew to a grumbling;

And the grumbling grew to a mighty rumbling;

And out of the houses the rats came tumbling.

Great rats, small rats, lean rats, brawny rats,

Brown rats, black rats, grey rats, tawny rats,

Grave old plodders, gay young friskers,

Fathers, mothers, uncles, cousins,

Cocking tails and pricking whiskers,

Families by tens and dozens,

Brothers, sisters, husbands, wives –

Followed the Piper for their lives.

From street to street he piped advancing,

And step for step they followed dancing,

Until they came to the river Weser,

Wherein all plunged and perished!

   * * *

Once more he stepped into the street

And to his lips again

Laid his long pipe of smooth straight cane;

And ere he blew three notes (such sweet

Soft notes as yet musician's cunning

Never gave the enraptured air)

There was a rustling that seemed like a bustling

Of merry crowds justling at pitching and hustling
Small feet were pattering, wooden shoes clattering,
Little hands clapping and little tongues chattering,
And, like fowls in a farmyard when barley is scattering,

Out came the children running.
All the little boys and girls,
With rosy cheeks and flaxen curls,
And sparkling eyes and teeth like pearls,
Tripping and skipping, ran merrily after
The wonderful music with shouting and laughter.

Robert Browning
1812–89, b. England

Browning wrote 'The Pied Piper of Hamelin' in 1842 to amuse the little son of one of his friends, so it is not typical of his poetry and he was at first reluctant to let it be published. The legend of the Pied Piper goes back to medieval times, a historical document recording that in 1284 the Piper, playing a haunting melody on his pipe, led away 130 children, who all vanished without a trace.

from The Lady of Shalott

Part I

On either side the river lie
Long fields of barley and of rye,
That clothe the wold and meet the sky;
And through the field the road runs by
To many-towered Camelot;
And up and down the people go,
Gazing where the lilies blow
Round an island there below,
The island of Shalott.

Willows whiten, aspens quiver,
Little breezes dusk and shiver
Through the wave that runs for ever
By the island in the river
Flowing down to Camelot.
Four gray walls, and four gray towers,
Overlook a space of flowers,
And the silent isle imbowers
The Lady of Shalott.

By the margin, willow-veiled,

Slide the heavy barges trailed

By slow horses; and unhailed

The shallop flitteth silken-sailed

Skimming down to Camelot:

But who hath seen her wave her hand?

Or at the casement seen her stand?

Or is she known in all the land,

The Lady of Shalott?

Only reapers, reaping early

In among the bearded barley,

Hear a song that echoes cheerly

From the river winding clearly,

Down to towered Camelot:

And by the moon the reaper weary,

Piling sheaves in uplands airy,

Listening, whispers ''Tis the fairy

Lady of Shalott.'

Part II

There she weaves by night and day
A magic web with colours gay.
She has heard a whisper say,
A curse is on her if she stay
To look down to Camelot.
She knows not what the curse may be,
And so she weaveth steadily,
And little other care hath she,
The Lady of Shalott.

And moving thro' a mirror clear
That hangs before her all the year,
Shadows of the world appear.
There she sees the highway near
Winding down to Camelot:
There the river eddy whirls,
And there the surly village-churls,
And the red cloaks of market girls,
Pass onward from Shalott.

Sometimes a troop of damsels glad,

An abbot on an ambling pad,

Sometimes a curly shepherd-lad,

Or long-hair'd page in crimson clad,

Goes by to towered Camelot;

And sometimes through the mirror blue

The knights come riding two and two:

She hath no loyal knight and true,

The Lady of Shalott.

But in her web she still delights

To weave the mirror's magic sights,

For often through the silent nights

A funeral, with plumes and lights,

And music, went to Camelot:

Or when the moon was overhead,

Came two young lovers lately wed;

'I am half sick of shadows,' said

The Lady of Shalott.

Alfred, Lord Tennyson
1809–92, b. England

*B*ased on an Arthurian myth of Lancelot and Elaine, Tennyson's heroine lives in a tower on an island, cursed to watch the world only in a looking glass and to weave what she sees. Captivated by the handsome Sir Lancelot's reflection, she goes to the window to see him and brings doom upon herself. She is able then to leave her prison and sail to the town, but she dies on the journey. The poem inspired a wonderful Pre-Raphaelite painting by Holman Hunt.

The Night is Darkening Round Me

The night is darkening round me,

The wild winds coldly blow;

But a tyrant spell has bound me

And I cannot, cannot go.

The giant trees are bending

Their bare boughs weighed with snow,

The storm is fast descending

And yet I cannot go.

Clouds beyond clouds above me,

Wastes beyond wastes below;

But nothing drear can move me;

I will not, cannot go.

Emily Brontë
1818–48, b. England

*E*mily Brontë loved her isolated home on the bleak Yorkshire moors with a passion. Her sisters, Charlotte and Anne, persuaded Emily to have a selection of their poems published pseudonymously in 1846 – only two copies were sold. The following year, Emily's novel Wuthering Heights was published with scant recognition, and in 1848 she died of tuberculosis. Today, Emily Brontë ranks among the greatest English poets and Wuthering Heights is considered to be a masterpiece.

Infant Sorrow

My mother groaned, my father wept,
Into the dangerous world I leapt;
Helpless, naked, piping loud,
Like a fiend hid in a cloud.

Struggling in my father's hands,
Striving against my swaddling bands,
Bound and weary, I thought best
To sulk upon my mother's breast.

William Blake
1757–1827, b. England

*T*his poem by William Blake appeared in a collection called Songs of Experience *which was* published in 1794. His famous poem 'The Tyger' *also appeared in this work. The poems are an observation from a child's point of view.*

The Kraken

Below the thunders of the upper deep;

Far, far beneath in the abysmal sea,

His ancient, dreamless, uninvaded sleep

The Kraken sleepeth: faintest sunlights flee

About his shadowy sides: above him swell

Huge sponges of millennial growth and height;

And far away into the sickly light,

From many a wondrous grot and secret cell

Unnumber'd and enormous polypi

Winnow with giant arms the slumbering green.

There hath he lain for ages and will lie

Battening upon huge seaworms in his sleep,

Until the latter fire shall heat the deep;

Then once by man and angels to be seen,

In roaring he shall rise and on the surface die.

Alfred, Lord Tennyson
1809–92, b. England

For thousands of years sailors have spoken of the kraken, a sea monster so strong it could kill a whale. They say it could possibly be a giant squid.

Tennyson's poem evokes a sense of an ominous threat lurking in the depths of the sea. He was only 21 when he wrote this poem in 1830.

Light Shining
out of Darkness

God moves in a mysterious way,
    His wonders to perform;
He plants his footsteps in the sea,
    And rides upon the storm.

Deep in unfathomable mines
    Of never failing skill,
He treasures up his bright designs,
    And works his sovereign will.

Ye fearful saints, fresh courage take,
    The clouds ye so much dread
Are big with mercy, and shall break
    In blessings on your head.

Judge not the Lord by feeble sense,
    But trust him for his grace;
Behind a frowning providence,
    He hides a smiling face.

His purposes will ripen fast,
  Unfolding every hour;
The bud may have a bitter taste,
  But sweet will be the flower.

Blind unbelief is sure to err,
  And scan his work in vain;
God is his own interpreter,
  And he will make it plain.

William Cowper
1731–1800, b. England

William Cowper was called to the Bar in 1754 but never practised Law. He suffered from delicate health and experienced recurrent bouts of depression, but his strong religious conviction and supportive friends helped him through. He was a poet and essayist and the first lines of the poem 'Light Shining out of Darkness' are much quoted.

Satan

…His Pride

Had cast him out from Heaven, with all his Host

Of Rebel Angels, by whose aid aspiring

To set himself in Glory above his Peers,

He trusted to have equalled the most High,

If he opposed; and with ambitious aim

Against the Throne and Monarchy of God

Raised impious War in Heaven and Battle proud

With vain attempt. Him the Almighty Power

Hurled headlong flaming from the Ethereal Sky

With hideous ruin and combustion down

To bottomless perdition, there to dwell

In Adamantine Chains and penal Fire,

Who durst defy the Omnipotent to Arms.

John Milton
1608–74, b. England

*T*his quotation is from Paradise Lost Book I, *one of the most influencial poems in English literature. John Milton dictated the poem and had sections read* back to him as he was blind by this time in his life. The poem was composed during the period from 1658 until 1667.

FOOD AND DRINK

⚬⚬⚬

The joys of eating and drinking and the very
fragrances of the ingredients themselves come
together here in a feast of poems that celebrate
food and drink. Swift's plump, fresh mussels,
Thackeray's tender and juicy leg of mutton,
Sydney Smith's simple salad recipe, Lewis Carroll's
mock turtle soup, Keats' 'beaker of the warm
South' and the 'Creams, and cordials, and sugared
dates' that Thomas Bailey Aldrich swoons for,
are just some of the delicacies that you will
find on the following pages.

I Gave My Love a Cherry

I gave my love a cherry
That has no stone,

I gave my love a chicken
That has no bone,

I gave my love a baby
That's no cryin'.

How can there be a cherry
That has no stone?

How can there be a chicken
That has no bone?

How can there be a baby
That's no cryin'?

A cherry when it's buddin',

It has no stone.

A chicken in the eggshell,

It has no bone.

A baby when it's sleepin',

Is no cryin'.

Old Appalachian song
Author unknown

The poem 'I Gave My Love a Cherry' comes from the Appalachian Mountains in the United States. It has a simple charm with its stanzas of questions and answers. The verses are also well known in a song version, although the author is unknown.

The Cook

A cook they hadde with hem for the nones

    They had a cook with them who stood alone

To boille the chiknes with the marybones,

    For boiling chicken with a marrow-bone,

And poudre-marchant tart, and galyngale.

    Sharp flavouring powder and a spice for savour.

Wel koude he knowe a draughte of London ale.

    He could distinguish London ale by flavour,

He koude rooste, and sethe, and broille, and frye,

    And he could roast and boil and seethe and fry,

Maken mortreux, and wel bake a pye.

    Make good thick soup and bake a tasty pie.

For blankmanger, that made he with the beste.

As for blancmange, he made it with the best.

Geoffrey Chaucer
1340?–1400?

The cook in this poem is one of the pilgrims, who tell their stories in Geoffrey Chaucer's The Canterbury Tales. *The pilgrims were on their way, one April day, to Canterbury to visit the shrine of the martyr St Thomas (á) Becket. The Canterbury Tales were written in English at a time when court poetry was usually written in Anglo-Norman or Latin and remained incomplete due to Chaucer's death in 1400.*

Cider Apples

When God had made the oak trees,

And the beeches and the pines,

And the flowers and the grasses,

And the tendrils of the vines;

He saw that there was wanting

A something in His plan,

And He made the little apples,

The little cider apples,

The sharp, sour cider apples,

To prove his love for man.

Author unknown

*C*ider apples are small, hard and inedible. Traditionally they are harvested by shaking the tree with a hooklug, a long hooked pole, and then picked up manually to transport to the mill for making into cider. This poem is another anonymous work handed down through time and has a hymnlike quality to it.

A Recipe for a Salad

To make this condiment, your poet begs

The pounded yellow of two hard-boiled eggs;

Two boiled potatoes, passed through kitchen sieve,

Smoothness and softness to the salad give.

Let onion atoms lurk within the bowl,

And, half suspected, animate the whole.

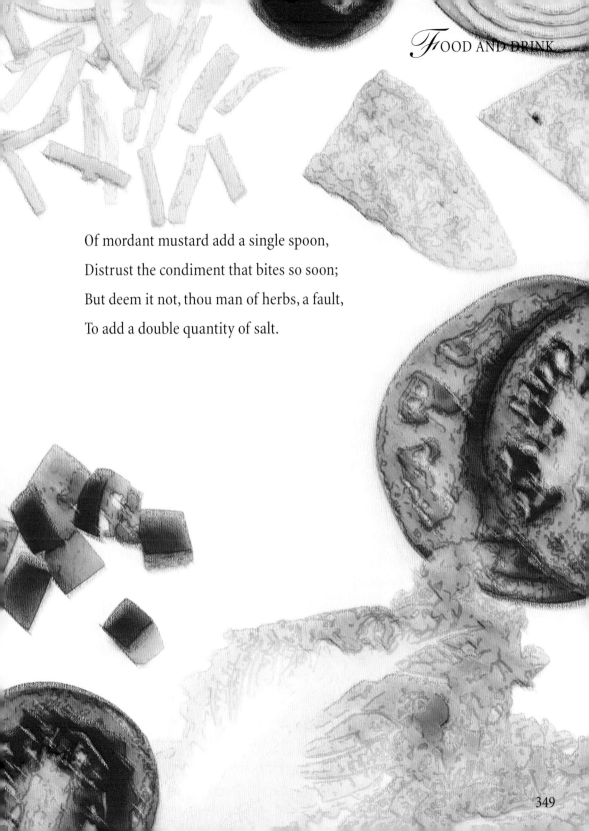

Of mordant mustard add a single spoon,

Distrust the condiment that bites so soon;

But deem it not, thou man of herbs, a fault,

To add a double quantity of salt.

Four times the spoon with oil from Lucca brown,

And twice with vinegar procured from town;

And, lastly, o'er the flavoured compound toss

A magic soupcion of anchovy sauce.

O, green and glorious! O herbaceous treat!

'T would tempt the dying anchorite to eat:

Back to the world he'd turn his fleeting soul,

And plunge his fingers in the salad bowl!

Serenely full, the epicure would say,

'Fate cannot harm me, I have dined to-day.'

Sydney Smith
1771–1845, b. England

Sydney Smith was a clergyman, essayist and writer. During a lifetime serving the Church he also co-founded and contributed to the Edinburgh Review, *published a book of sermons, wrote letters and occasional verse and lectured in moral philosophy at the Royal Institution. He had a reputation as an outstandingly witty preacher.*

One Potato

One potato,

Two potato,

Three potato,

Four;

Five potato,

Six potato,

Seven potato,

More;

Bad one out!

Traditional rhyme

*T*he chant 'One potato, Two potato' has been heard in the playground for generations. It is another of the anonymous counting rhymes which have been a useful and unconscious way of learning numbers.

To Make a Good Chowder

To make a good chowder and have it quite nice

Dispense with sweet marjoram, parsley and spice;

Mace, pepper and salt are now wanted alone.

To make the stew eat well and stick to the bone,

Some pork is sliced thin and put into the pot;

Some say you must turn it, some say you must not;

And when it is brown, take it out of the fat,

And add it again when you add this and that.

A layer of potatoes, sliced quarter inch thick,

Should be placed in the bottom to make it eat slick;

A layer of onions now over this place,

Then season with pepper and salt and some mace.

Split open your crackers and give them a soak;

In eating you'll find this the cream of the joke.

On top of all this, now comply with my wish

And put in large chunks, all your pieces of fish;

Then put on the pieces of pork you have fried

I mean those from which all the fat has been tried.

In seasoning I pray you, don't spare the cayenne;

'Tis this makes it fit to be eaten by men.

After adding these things in their regular rotation

You'll have a dish fit for the best of the nation.

Author unknown

In 'To Make a Good Chowder' the unknown author cleverly makes a recipe rhyme. A chowder is a satisfying soup that is said to take its name from the large, French, three-legged iron cooking pot known as a chaudiére. The dish is unpretentious and improves by its flexible use of ingredients each time it is made.

Beautiful Soup

Beautiful soup, so rich and green,

Waiting in a hot tureen!

Who for such dainties would not stoop?

Soup of the evening, beautiful Soup!

Soup of the evening, beautiful Soup!

Beau—ootiful Soo–oop!

Beau—ootiful Soo-oop!

Soo—oop of the e-e-evening,

Beautiful, beautiful Soup!

Beautiful Soup! Who cares for fish,

Game, or any other dish?

Who would not give all else for two

Pennyworth only of Beautiful Soup?

Pennyworth only of beautiful Soup?

Beau—ootiful Soo-oop!

Beau—ootiful Soo-oop!

Soo—oop of the e-e-evening,

Beautiful, beauti—FUL SOUP!

Lewis Carroll
1832–98, b. England

Mock turtle soup is an English soup created as a substitute for the more expensive turtle soup in the mid-18th-century. The Mock Turtle sobs as he tells Alice that he was once a real turtle and sings this song to her in Chapter 10 of Alice's Adventures in Wonderland.

Some Hae Meat

Some hae meat and canna eat,

And some wad eat that want it;

But we hae meat, and we can eat,

And sae the Lord be thankit.

Robert Burns

1759–96, b. Scotland

Burns Night is celebrated each year on January 25 in honour of the great Scottish poet Robert Burns. After Burns died in 1796, a group of his close friends established the Burns Night Supper as a tribute to his memory. During the celebrations, tradition dictates the recital of the 'Selkirk Prayer' or 'Some Hae Meat' after the haggis has been received by the company.

Onions

'This is every cook's opinion –

No savory dish without an onion,

But lest your kissing should be spoiled

Your onions must be fully boiled.'

Jonathan Swift
1667–1745, b. Ireland

Some say onions originated in Central Asia, others suggest they were first grown in Iran and West Pakistan. They are thought to have been a staple in the prehistoric diet and were Egyptian objects of worship. Onions are upheld as remedies for all sorts of ailments. Swift's witty little poem suggests that they are better cooked – from a social point of view!

from Ode to a Nightingale

O, for a draught of vintage! that hath been

Cool'd a long age in the deep-delv'd earth,

Tasting of Flora and the country-green,

Dance, and Provencal song, and sunburnt mirth!

Oh, for a beaker of the warm South,

Full of the true, the blushful Hippocrene,

With beaded bubbles winking at the brim,

And purple-stained mouth;

That I might drink and leave the world unseen,

And with thee fade away into the forest dim.

John Keats
1795–1821, b. England

John Keats composed the poem 'Ode to a Nightingale' in 1818 after a nightingale built its nest near his house. In the second verse of the poem he evokes the pleasure of drinking a draught of full-bodied wine. Keats died very young and yet was the author of 150 poems. He is considered one of the finest English lyric poets.

Mix a Pancake

Mix a Pancake,

Stir a Pancake,

Pop it in the pan;

Fry the pancake,

Toss the pancake –

Catch it if you can.

Christina Rossetti
1830–94, b. England

*L*arge, small, wafer-thin or fat, and made with a wide variety of flours, pancakes are given different names in countries around the world. Nobody knows how long people have been making pancakes. Christina Rossetti will have enjoyed them at the onset of Lent, when surplus supplies of fat and eggs were used up.

Persicos Odi

Dear Lucy, you know what my wish is,
    I hate all your Frenchified fuss:
Your silly entrées and made dishes
    Were never intended for us.

No footman in lace and in ruffles
    Need dangle behind my arm-chair;
And never mind seeking for truffles,
    Although they be ever so rare.

But a plain leg of mutton, my Lucy,
    I pr'ythee get ready at three:
Have it smoking, and tender, and juicy,
    And what better meat can here be?

And when it has feasted the master,

'Twill amply suffice for the maid;

Meanwhile I will smoke my canaster,

And tipple my ale in the shade.

William Makepeace Thackeray

1811–63, b. India

William Makepeace Thackeray was known as a humorous writer. Born in Calcutta and educated in England, he left Cambridge University without his degree and tried careers in law and as an artist before becoming a writer. The poem's title is taken from the writings of the Roman philosopher and drama critic, Horace.

There on a Slope
of Orchard

There on a slope of orchard, Francis laid

A damask napkin wrought with horse and hound,

brought out a dusky loaf that smelt of home,

And half-cut-down, a pasty costly made,

Where quail and pigeon, lark and leveret, lay

Like fossils of the rock, with golden yolks

Imbedded and injellied.

Alfred, Lord Tennyson
1809–92, b. England

*T*he lines by Alfred, Lord Tennyson in the verse 'There on a Slope of Orchard' evoke an image of a picnic of tasty foods eaten in the sweet air in an orchard on a warm day. The food could be from much earlier than Tennyson's lifetime and from any of a number of countries, but utterly delicious.

When the Sultan Goes to Ispahan

When the Sultan Shah-Zaman

Goes to the city Ispahan,

Even before he gets so far

As the place where the clustered palm-trees are,

At the last of the thirty palace-gates

The pet of the harem, Rose-in-Bloom,

Orders a feast in his favourite room –

Glittering square of coloured ice,

Sweetened with syrup, tinctured with spice,

Creams, and cordials, and sugared dates,

Syrian apples, Othmanee quinces,

Limes and citrons and apricots,

And wines that are known to Eastern princes.

Thomas Bailey Aldrich
1836–1907, b. USA

Thomas Bailey Aldrich was hailed as father of the American novel. He was an editor and contributor to many magazines, and a poet. His poem 'When the Sultan Goes to Ispahan' *conjures up the colour, atmosphere and flavours of an exotic city of long ago. Ispahan is in modern-day Iran.*

Oysters

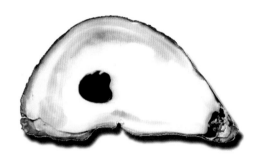

Charming oysters I cry:

My masters, come buy,

So plump and so fresh,

So sweet is their flesh,

No Colchester oyster

Is sweeter and moister:

Your stomach they settle,

And rouse up your mettle:

They'll make you a dad

Of a lass or a lad;

And madam your wife

They'll please to the life;

Be she barren, be she old,

Be she slut, or be she scold,

Eat my oysters, and lie near her,

She'll be fruitful, never fear her.

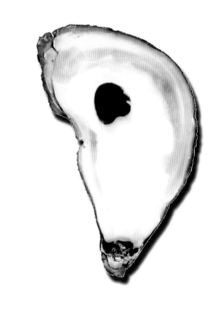

Jonathan Swift
1667–1745, b. Ireland

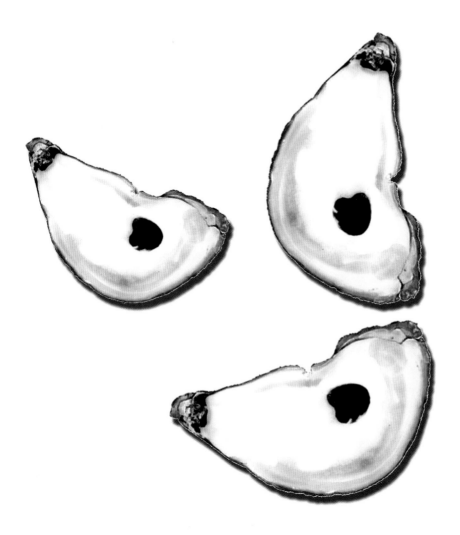

*I*n the world of cooking and eating there are many myths and legends about different foods. Throughout history, various foods have been thought to have aphrodisiac qualities. Figs, truffles, radishes, asparagus and oysters are just some. Jonathan Swift's poem about the oyster alludes to their possible effects.

Christmas Cheer

Good husband and huswife, now chiefly be glad,

Things handsome to have, as they ought to be had.

They both do provide, against Christmas do come,

To welcome their neighbours, good cheer to have some.

Good bread and good drink, a good fire in the hall,

Brawn, pudding, and souse, and good mustard withal.

Beef, mutton, and pork, and good pies of the best,

Pig, veal, goose, and capon, and turkey well drest,

Cheese, apples and nuts, and good carols to hear,

As then in the country is counted good cheer.

What cost to good husband, is any of this?

Good household provision only it is:

Of other the like, I do leave out a many,

That costeth the husband never a penny.

Thomas Tusser
1524?–80, b. England

*T*homas Tusser wrote 'Christmas Cheer' in the 16th century. It evokes the traditional image of the table laden with all the delicious food of Christmas time. Tusser had a fine voice and was a chorister at St Paul's and Norwich Cathedral. As a farmer he was unsuccessful but he wrote some fine verses on agriculture.

To a Goose

If thou didst feed on western plains of yore;

Or waddle wide with flat and flabby feet

Over some Cambrian mountain's plashy moor;

Or find in farmer's yard a safe retreat

From gipsy thieves, and foxes sly and fleet;

If thy grey quills, by lawyer guided, trace

Deeds big with ruin to some wretched race,

Or love-sick poet's sonnet, sad and sweet,

Wailing the rigour of his lady fair;

Or if, the drudge of housemaid's daily toil,

Cobwebs and dust thy pinions white besoil,

Departed Goose! I neither know nor care.

But this I know, that thou wert very fine,

Season'd with sage and onions, and port wine.

Robert Southey
1774–1843, b. England

*I*n his youth Robert Southey was a radical figure. He and the poet Samuel Taylor Coleridge joined forces with the idea of forming a pantisocracy, a utopian community, in America. They abandoned the plan but remained friends and married two sisters. Southey produced a large body of work in his lifetime and was Poet Laureate for 30 years. He was succeeded by William Wordsworth.

Camomile Tea

Outside the sky is light with stars;

There's a hollow roaring from the sea.

And, alas! for the little almond flowers,

The wind is shaking the almond tree.

How little I thought, a year ago,

In the horrible cottage upon the Lee

That he and I should be sitting so

And sipping a cup of camomile tea.

Light as feathers the witches fly,

The horn of the moon is plain to see;

By a firefly under a jonquil flower

A goblin toasts a bumble-bee.

We might be fifty, we might be five,

So snug, so compact, so wise are we!

Under the kitchen-table leg

My knee is pressing against his knee.

Our shutters are shut, the fire is low,

The tap is dripping peacefully;

The saucepan shadows on the wall

Are black and round and plain to see.

Katherine Mansfield
1888–1917, b. New Zealand

*K*atherine Mansfield pursued her literary career in London where she mixed with a bohemian set. She shared a tempestuous relationship with John Middleton Murry, the essayist and critic, and with him mixed with some of the leading lights in English literature. D H Lawrence was a friend. He based the characters Gudrun and Gerald in Women in Love on Mansfield and Murry. Katherine Mansfield died young of tuberculosis.

Muffin Man

Oh, do you know the muffin man,

The muffin man, the muffin man?

Oh, do you know the muffin man,

That lives in Drury Lane?

Yes, I know the muffin man,

The muffin man, the muffin man.

Yes, I know the muffin man,

That lives in Drury Lane.

Traditional rhyme

Simple Simon

Simple Simon met a pieman going to the fair;

Said Simple Simon to the pieman 'Let me taste your ware.'

Said the pieman to Simple Simon 'Show me first

your penny.'

Said Simple Simon to the pieman 'Sir, I have not any!'

Traditional rhyme

Both of these well-loved nursery rhymes date back to medieval times when all types of foods would be sold at fairs or in the streets. The different street sellers would have a special cry to attract attention to sell their wares. The authors are unknown.

I Wonder if the Cabbage Knows

I wonder if the cabbage knows

He is less lovely than the Rose;

Or does he squat in smug content,

A source of noble nourishment;

Or if he pities for her sins

The Rose who has no vitamins;

Or if the one thing his green heart knows –

That self-same fire that warms the Rose?

Author unknown

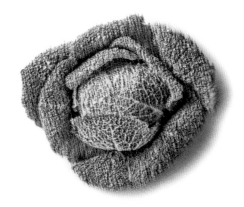

*I*t could be argued that both the cabbage and the rose are beautiful plants in their own right, and in fact there is a type of rose called a cabbage rose. Cabbages have been cultivated for over 4000 years and have become a staple in our diet. Roses are one of the oldest flowers known to man and are the flower of love.

NATURE

Keats' 'Endymion' begins 'A thing of beauty is a joy for ever', and this could well be said of the huge treasury of poems that the theme of nature has brought to the world, inspiring as it has, some of the finest lines from a wide range of writers. Among those writers featured in this section are William Wordsworth, Christina Rossetti, Matthew Arnold, John Keats, Emily Dickinson, Leigh Hunt, William Shakespeare and John Clare.

from The Prelude

One summer evening (led by her) I found

A little boat tied to a willow tree

Within a rocky cave, its usual home.

Straight I unloosed her chain, and stepping in

Pushed from the shore. It was an act of stealth

And troubled pleasure, nor without the voice

Of mountain-echoes did my boat move on;

Leaving behind her still, on either side,

Small circles glittering idly in the moon,

Until they melted all into one track

Of sparkling light . . .

. . . I dipped my oars into the silent lake,

And, as I rose upon the stroke, my boat

Went heaving through the water like a swan;

When, from behind that craggy steep till then

The horizon's bound, a huge peak, black and huge,

As if with voluntary power instinct

Upreared its head. I struck and struck again,

And growing still in stature the grim shape

Towered up between me and the stars, and still,

For so it seemed, with purpose of its own

And measured motion like a living thing,

Strode after me ...

William Wordsworth
1770–1850, b. England

Wordsworth wrote a two-part version of The Prelude *in 1799, completed a 13-book draft in 1805, and then revised it several times (a 14-book form was published posthumously in 1850). In it, Wordsworth remembers the key experiences from his life, especially* childhood, that shaped his poetic imagination. This extract has a chilling darkness at its core. He described the huge, autobiographical work as 'the Growth of a Poet's Mind' – which was a highly original choice of subject.*

The Windhover

To Christ Our Lord

I caught this morning morning's minion, kingdom
   of daylight's dauphin, dapple-dawn-drawn Falcon,
      in his riding
   Of the rolling level underneath him steady air,
      and striding
High there, how he rung upon the rein of a wimpling wing
In his ecstasy! then off, off forth on swing,
   As a skate's heel sweeps smooth on a bow-bend;
      the hurl and gliding
   Rebuffed the big wind. My heart in hiding
Stirred for a bird, – the achieve of, the mastery of the thing!

Brute beauty and valour and act, oh, air, pride, plume, here
   Buckle! AND the fire that breaks from thee then, a billion
Times told lovelier, more dangerous, O my chevalier!

No wonder of it: shèer plòd makes plough down sillion

Shine, and blue-bleak embers, ah my dear,

    Fall, gall themselves, and gash gold-vermilion.

Gerard Manley Hopkins
1844–89, b. England

Hopkins was a priest who struggled to reconcile his acute sense of God's hand in nature with the religious doctrine that the natural world is fallen. Here, a soaring windhover (kestrel) resembles Christ on the cross. Hopkins marvels at the bird's mastery of the air, but finds it is the moment when the wind overcomes the bird that is the most magnificent. Earth is most beautiful when broken by the plough, and embers when they disintegrate. For Hopkins, nature is reflecting the glory of Christ's death.

from The Song of Hiawatha

At the door on summer evenings

Sat the little Hiawatha;

Heard the whispering of the pine-trees,

Heard the lapping of the water,

Sounds of music, words of wonder;

'Minne-wawa!' said the pine-trees,

'Mudway-aushka!' said the water.

Saw the firefly, Wah-wah-taysee,

Flitting through the dusk of evening,

With the twinkle of its candle

Lighting up the brakes and bushes;

And he sang the song of children,

Sang the song Nokomis taught him:

'Wah-wah-taysee, little firefly,

Little, flitting, white-fire insect,

Little, dancing, white-fire creature,

Light me with your little candle,

Ere upon my bed I lay me,

Ere in sleep I close my eyelids!'

Henry Wadsworth Longfellow

1807–82, b. USA

There was once a real Hiawatha (he lived in the 15th century and was chief of the Onondaga tribe of Iroquois Native Americans), and his heroic achievements have become the magical stuff of legend. Longfellow's

The Song of Hiawatha *(1858) popularized the folklore of the original inhabitants of America. Longfellow is the only American to be honoured with a bust in the Poets' Corner of Westminster Abbey.*

from Endymion

A thing of beauty is a joy for ever:

Its loveliness increases; it will never

Pass into nothingness, but still will keep

A bower quiet for us, and a sleep

Full of sweet dreams, and health, and quiet breathing.

Therefore, on every morrow, are we wreathing

A flowery band to bind us to the earth,

Spite of despondence, of the inhuman dearth

Of noble natures, of the gloomy days,

Of all the unhealthy and o'er-darkened ways

Made for our searching – yes, in spite of all,

Some shape of beauty moves away the pall

From our dark spirits. Such the sun, the moon,

Trees, old and young, sprouting a shady boon

For simple sheep; and such are daffodils

With the green world they live in; and clear rills

That for themselves a cooling covert make

'Gainst the hot season; the mid-forest brake,

Rich with a sprinkling of fair musk-rose blooms;

And such too is the grandeur of the dooms

We have imagined for the mighty dead,

All lovely tales that we have heard or read –

An endless fountain of immortal drink,

Pouring unto us from the heaven's brink.

John Keats
1795–1822, b. England

John Keats is regarded as one of the main poets of the Romantic movement. 'Endymion', published in 1818, was his longest work, and tells the Greek legend of a shepherd called Endymion who falls in love with the goddess Cynthia. The poem was originally slammed by the critic Lockhart as 'drivelling idiocy'! Keats was deeply hurt, but wrote courageously, 'I think I shall be among the English poets after my death.'

What Does the Bee Do?

What does the bee do?

What does the bee do?

   Bring home honey.

And what does Father do?

   Bring home money.

And what does Mother do?

   Lay out the money.

And what does baby do?

   Eat up the honey.

Christina Rossetti
1830–94, b. England

This poem appeared in the collection of Christina Rossetti's nursery rhymes called Sing-Song published in 1872. The poem is written in a circular way starting with the father, like the busy bee, going out to work and returning home with the money to buy the baby's honey.

Daffodils

I wander'd lonely as a cloud
That floats on high o'er vales and hills,
When all at once I saw a crowd,
A host of golden daffodils,
Beside the lake, beneath the trees
Fluttering and dancing in the breeze.

Continuous as the stars that shine
And twinkle on the milky way,
They stretch'd in never-ending line
Along the margin of a bay:
Ten thousand saw I at a glance
Tossing their heads in sprightly dance.

The waves beside them danced, but they
Out-did the sparkling waves in glee: –
A Poet could not but be gay
In such a jocund company!
I gazed – and gazed – but little thought
What wealth the show to me had brought.

For oft, when on my couch I lie

In vacant or in pensive mood,

They flash upon that inward eye

Which is the bliss of solitude;

And then my heart with pleasure fills

And dances with the daffodils.

William Wordsworth
1770–1850, b. England

Wordsworth grew up in the wild beauty of Cumbria. After travelling to Italy and France, he lived in Dorset and Somerset, before returning to his beloved Lake District. Many of his poems describe uplifting moments of joy that suddenly came upon him when he was on his own amidst nature. The sense of peace and permanence he experienced in the natural world were proof to him that all things – even human poverty and tragedy – were part of a harmonious creation.

from Dover Beach

The sea is calm tonight.

The tide is full, the moon lies fair

Upon the straits; – on the French coast the light

Gleams and is gone; the cliffs of England stand,

Glimmering and vast, out in the tranquil bay.

Come to the window, sweet is the night-air!

Only, from the long line of spray

Where the sea meets the moon-blanched land,

Listen! you hear the grating roar

Of pebbles which the waves draw back, and fling,

At their return, up the high strand,

Begin, and cease, and then again begin,

With tremulous cadence slow, and bring

The eternal note of sadness in.

Matthew Arnold

1822–88, b. England

*P*art of 'Dover Beach' dates from Matthew Arnold's honeymoon, when he stayed at Dover. He was a schools inspector by profession, who travelled extensively throughout England for 15 years and campaigned for improved education and social conditions. After writing several volumes of poetry, Arnold turned in later life to writing critical essays, becoming the leading critic of his day.

To Autumn

Season of mists and mellow fruitfulness,
    Close bosom-friend of the maturing sun;
Conspiring with him how to load and bless
    With fruit the vines that round the thatch-eaves run;
To bend with apples the mossed cottage-trees,
    And fill all fruit with ripeness to the core;
      To swell the gourd, and plump the hazel shells
    With a sweet kernel; to set budding more,
And still more, later flowers for the bees,
Until they think warm days will never cease,
    For Summer has o'er-brimmed their clammy cells.

Who hath not seen thee oft amid thy store?

Sometimes whoever seeks abroad may find

Thee sitting careless on a granary floor,

Thy hair soft-lifted by the winnowing wind;

Or on a half-reaped furrow sound asleep,

Drowsed with the fume of poppies, while thy hook

Spares the next swath and all its twinèd flowers:

And sometimes like a gleaner thou dost keep

Steady thy laden head across a brook;

Or by a cider-press, with patient look,

Thou watchest the last oozings, hours

by hours.

Where are the songs of Spring? Ay, where are they?

    Think not of them, thou hast thy music too –

While barrèd clouds bloom the soft-dying day,

    And touch the stubble-plains with rosy hue;

Then in a wailful choir the small gnats mourn

    Among the river sallows, borne aloft

      Or sinking as the light wind lives or dies;

    And full-grown lambs loud bleat from hilly bourn;

Hedge-crickets sing; and now with treble soft

The red-breast whistles from a garden croft;

    And gathering swallows twitter in the skies.

John Keats
1795–1822, b. England

Keats abandoned his apothecary's licence aged 21 for poetry. However, he composed his greatest poems in just one year of his writing career, at a time when he was beset by financial problems and ill health! Beginning in September 1818, Keats wrote 'The Eve of St Agnes', his famous 'Odes, La Belle Dame sans Merci', and 'Lamia', among others. 'To Autumn' was Keats' last major poem, written in September 1819. It celebrates the abundance of the season and mourns the passing of summer.

A Slash of Blue

A slash of Blue –

A sweep of Grey –

Some scarlet patches on the way,

Compose an Evening Sky –

A little purple – slipped between

Some Ruby Trousers hurried on –

A Wave of Gold –

A Bank of Day –

This just makes out the Morning Sky.

Emily Dickinson
1830–86, b. USA

From a distinguished family and educated at a foremost women's college, Emily Dickinson shut herself inside her house for increasing periods until eventually she wouldn't leave home at all and refused to see nearly everybody. After her death, her sister found a box containing almost 2000 poems – some in carefully hand-stiched books, others scrawled onto scraps. They were finally published and Emily Dickinson is now considered to be one of the greatest American poets.

To a Fish

You strange, astonished-looking, angle-faced,

Dreary-mouthed, gaping wretches of the sea,

Gulping salt-water everlastingly,

Cold-blooded, though with red your blood be graced,

And mute, though dwellers in the roaring waste;

And you, all shapes beside, that fishy be, –

Some round, some flat, some long, all devilry,

Legless, unloving, infamously chaste: –

O scaly, slippery, wet, swift, staring wights,

What is't ye do? What life lead? eh, dull goggles?

How do ye vary your vile days and nights?

How pass your Sundays? Are ye still but joggles

In ceaseless wash? Still nought but gapes, and bites,

And drinks, and stares, diversified with boggles?

Leigh Hunt
1784–1859, b. England

L *eigh Hunt was an important figure in the world of literature in the 19th century. As the owner of various magazines he was responsible for promoting emerging writers like Keats, Shelley and Tennyson. Charles Dickens immortalized him as the character Skimpole in his book* Bleak House. *Hunt's graphic poem about a fish is one of many poems written during his eventful lifetime.*

It Was a Lover and His Lass

It was a lover and his lass,
With a hey, and a ho, and a hey nonino,
That o'er the green corn-field did pass,
In the spring time, the only pretty ring time,
When birds do sing, hey ding a ding, ding;
Sweet lovers love the spring.

Between the acres of the rye,
With a hey, and a ho, and a hey nonino,
These pretty country folks would lie,
In the spring time, the only pretty ring time,
When birds do sing, hey ding a ding, ding;
Sweet lovers love the spring.

This carol they began that hour,
With a hey, and a ho, and a hey nonino,
How that life was but a flower
In the spring time, the only pretty ring time,
When birds do sing, hey ding a ding, ding;
Sweet lovers love the spring.

And, therefore, take the present time

With a hey, and a ho, and a hey nonino,

For love is crownèd with the prime

In the spring time, the only pretty ring time,

When birds do sing, hey ding a ding, ding;

Sweet lovers love the spring.

William Shakespeare

1564–1616, b. England

The lyrical love poem 'It Was a Lover and His Lass' comes from Shakespeare's comedy, As You Like It. The play was written in London around 1600 and set in the most part in 16th-century France. Events take place in the pastoral setting of the Forest of Arden with random encounters between characters.

from A Thaw

The snow is gone from cottage tops

The thatch moss glows in brighter green

And eves in quick succession drops

Where grinning ides once hath been

Pit patting Wi a pleasant noise

In tubs set by the cottage door

And ducks and geese wi happy joys

Douse in the yard pond brimming oer

The sun peeps thro the window pane

Which childern mark wi laughing eye

And in the wet street steal again

To tell each other spring is nigh

And as young hope the past recalls

In playing groups will often draw

Building beside the sunny walls

Their spring-play-huts of sticks or straw

John Clare
1793–1864, b. England

John Clare was a working man all his life. He scraped a living in the Northampton countryside, sometimes working as a haymaker, lime-burner or gardener. As he walked through the local fields he would compose his poems. Clare's style of rural poetry brought him brief celebrity status in London but fashions changed and he suffered mental anguish and poverty.

The Lincolnshire Poacher

When I was bound apprentice in famous Lincolnshire,
Full well I served my master for more than seven years,
Till I took up to poaching, as you shall quickly hear,
Oh, 'tis my delight on a shiny night in the season of the year.

As me and my companions were setting of a snare,
'Twas then we spied the gamekeeper, for him we did not care,
For we can wrestle and fight, my boys and jump out anywhere,
Oh, 'tis my delight on a shiny night in the season of the year.

As me and my companions were setting four or five,
And taking on 'em up again, we caught a hare alive.
We took a hare alive my boys, and through the woods did steer
Oh, 'tis my delight on a shiny night in the season of the year.

I threw him on my shoulder and then we trudged home

We took him to a neighbour's house, and sold him for a crown;

We sold him for a crown, my boys, but I did not tell you where

Oh, 'tis my delight on a shiny night in the season of the year.

Success to ev'ry gentleman that lives in Lincolnshire

Success to every poacher that wants to sell a hare

Bad luck to ev'ry gamekeeper that will not sell his deer

Oh, 'tis my delight on a shiny night in the season of the year.

Author unknown

This ballad dates back to the 18th century. The oldest printed copy of it was made in York in about 1776. It is reputed to have been a great favourite of King George IV (1762–1830), who had it sung to him by a band of Berkshire ploughmen.

To a Mouse

Wee, sleekit, cowrin, tim'rous beastie,

O, what a panic's in thy breastie!

Thou need na start awa sae hasty,

Wi' bickering brattle!

I wad be laith to rin an' chase thee,

Wi' murd'ring pattle!

I'm truly sorry Man's dominion

Has broken Nature's social union,

An' justifies that ill opinion,

Which makes thee startle

At me, thy poor, earth-born companion,

An' fellow-mortal!

I doubt na, whiles, but thou may thieve;

What then? poor beastie, thou maun live!

A daimen icker in a thrave

'S a sma' request:

I'll get a blessin wi' the lave,

An' never miss't!

Thy wee-bit housie, too, in ruin!

It's silly wa's the win's are strewin!

An' naething, now, to big a new ane,

O' foggage green!

An' bleak December's winds ensuin,

Baith snell an' keen!

Thou saw the fields laid bare an' wast,

An' weary Winter comin fast,

An' cozie here, beneath the blast,

Thou thought to dwell –

Till crash! the cruel coulter past

Out thro' thy cell.

That wee-bit heap o' leaves an' stibble,

Has cost thee monie a weary nibble!

Now thou's turn'd out, for a' thy trouble,

But house or hald.

To thole the Winter's sleety dribble,

An' cranreuch cauld!

But Mousie, thou are no thy lane,

In proving foresight may be vain:

The best laid schemes o' Mice an' Men,

Gang aft agley,

An' lea'e us nought but grief an' pain,

For promis'd joy!

Still, thou art blest, compar'd wi' me!

The present only toucheth thee:

But och! I backward cast my e'e,

On prospects drear!

An' forward, tho' I canna see,

I guess an' fear!

Robert Burns

1759–96, b. Scotland

Robert Burns earned a living from farming and was known as the 'Ploughman Bard'. It was whilst ploughing one of his fields he disturbed a mouse's nest and was moved to write this tender poem.

My Garden

A garden is a lovesome thing, God wot!

Rose plot,

Fringed pool,

Ferned grot –

The veriest school

Of peace; and yet the fool

Contends that God is not –

Not God! in gardens! when the eve is cool?

Nay, but I have a sign:

'Tis very sure God walks in mine.

Thomas Edward Brown
1830–97, b. Isle of Man

Thomas Edward Brown was a writer and scholar and was ordained in 1856. Brown worked as a schoolmaster. He was the author of many poems written in the Manx dialect using a narrative style and irregular rhythms. This lovely poem 'My Garden' shows his enthusiastic appreciation of nature.

Adlestrop

Yes. I remember Adlestrop –
The name, because one afternoon
Of heat the express-train drew up there
Unwontedly. It was late June.

The steam hissed. Someone cleared his throat.
No one left and no one came
On the bare platform. What I saw
Was Adlestrop – only the name

And willows, willow-herb, and grass,
And meadowsweet, and haycocks dry,
No whit less still and lonely fair
Than the high cloudlets in the sky.

And for that minute a blackbird sang

Close by, and round him, mistier,

Farther and farther, all the birds

Of Oxfordshire and Gloucestershire.

Edward Thomas
1878–1917, b. England

*E*dward Thomas had a great love of the countryside, which was a theme of many of his poems. He made his living writing books, mainly about English country life, plus biographies and criticism. In 1913, Thomas met the American poet Robert Frost, who encouraged him to write poetry. Thomas is known for his poems written during World War I and was killed in action in Arras, France in 1917.

All Things Bright and Beautiful

Refrain:
All things bright and beautiful,
All creatures great and small,
All things wise and wonderful:
The Lord God made them all.

Each little flower that opens,
Each little bird that sings,
God made their glowing colours,
And made their tiny wings.

(Refrain)

The purple-headed mountains,
The river running by,
The sunset and the morning
That brightens up the sky.

(Refrain)

The cold wind in the winter,
The pleasant summer sun,
The ripe fruits in the garden:
God made them every one.

(Refrain)

God gave us eyes to see them,
And lips that we might tell
How great is God Almighty,
Who has made all things well.

Cecil Frances Alexander
1818–95, b. England

Cecil Frances Alexander was the author of nearly 400 hymns. 'All Things Bright and Beautiful' remains one of her best-known hymns and was written to explain the opening words of the Apostles' Creed, a Christian statement of belief. Cecil Frances Alexander was a devout woman and her life was deeply tied to the Church.

WEATHER AND SEASONS

―――――∝∝∝∝――――

A taste of the lines and poems in this section: 'London Snow': 'When men were all asleep the snow came flying'; 'Autumn Within': when 'Youth and spring are all about;/It is I that have grown old.'; 'Rhyme about Maytime' when 'a swarm of bees in May/ Is worth a load of hay'; 'The Sun Rising' like a 'Busy old fool'; 'A Rainy Day in April' when 'the rain/Like holy water falls upon the plain'; and 'Spring': 'When weeds, in wheels, shoot long and lovely and lush'.

London Snow

When men were all asleep the snow came flying,
In large white flakes falling on the city brown,
Stealthily and perpetually settling and loosely lying,
Hushing the latest traffic of the drowsy town;
Deadening, muffling, stifling its murmurs failing;
Lazily and incessantly floating down and down:
Silently sifting and veiling road, roof and railing;
Hiding difference, making unevenness even,
Into angles and crevices softly drifting and sailing.
All night it fell, and when full inches seven
It lay in the depth of its uncompacted lightness,
The clouds blew off from a high and frosty heaven;
And all woke earlier for the unaccustomed brightness
Of the winter dawning, the strange unheavenly glare:
The eye marvelled – marvelled at the dazzling whiteness;
The ear hearkened to the stillness of the solemn air;
No sound of wheel rumbling nor of foot falling,
And the busy morning cries came thin and spare.
Then boys I heard, as they went to school, calling,
They gathered up the crystal manna to freeze

Their tongues with tasting, their hands with snowballing;

Or rioted in a drift, plunging up to the knees;

Or peering up from under the white-mossed wonder,

'O look at the trees!' they cried, 'O look at the trees!'

With lessened load a few carts creak and blunder,

Following along the white deserted way,

A country company long dispersed asunder:

When now already the sun, in pale display

Standing by Paul's high dome, spread forth below

His sparkling beams, and awoke the stir of the day.

For now doors open, and war is waged with the snow;

And trains of sombre men, past tale of number,

Tread long brown paths, as toward their toil they go:

But even for them awhile no cares encumber

Their minds diverted; the daily word is unspoken,

The daily thoughts of labour and sorrow slumber

At the sight of the beauty that greets them,

For the charm they have broken.

Robert Bridges
1844–1930, b. England

*R*obert Bridges travelled extensively and studied and practised medicine in his early years. He wrote delicate and beautiful poems and was an influential literary figure in the early 20th century.

The poem 'London Snow' creates a wonderful picture of a fresh white snowfall and the muffled sounds of the city street.

from The Earthly Paradise

Folk say, a wizard to a northern king

At Christmas-tide such wondrous things did show,

That through one window men beheld the spring,

And through another saw the summer glow,

And through a third the fruited vines a-row,

While still, unheard, but in its wonted way,

Piped the drear wind of that December day.

William Morris
1834–96, b. England

William Morris was a man of many talents. He was a political activist and social thinker and a very important figure in the decorative arts. In 1890 he founded the Kelmscott Press where he designed his own typefaces and printed high quality editions of classic works. Morris wrote poetry throughout his life and The Earthly Paradise was published in parts between 1868 and 1870.

Autumn Within

It is autumn; not without

But within me is the cold.

Youth and spring are all about;

It is I that have grown old.

Birds are darting through the air,

Singing, building without rest;

Life is stirring everywhere,

Save within my lonely breast.

There is silence: the dead leaves

Fall and rustle and are still;

Beats no flail upon the sheaves,

Comes no murmur from the mill.

Henry Wadsworth Longfellow
1807–82, b. USA

Longfellow was a wonderful communicator and teacher, bringing different countries and people to his readers through his poems. As a youth he travelled from his home in America throughout much of Europe, learning many languages on his way. His poems are written with an easy rhyme and have obvious themes with a wide appeal. 'Autumn Within' creates a sad atmosphere using strong imagery.

Rhyme about Maytime

A swarm of bees in May

Is worth a load of hay;

A swarm of bees in June

Is worth a silver spoon;

A swarm of bees in July

Is not worth a fly.

Traditional rhyme

Before the days of scientific weather forecasting country folk had to keep a weather eye open to predict what conditions were going to be in store for them. Watching the clouds, the colour of the sky and the movement of birds might have helped them in their weather predictions. Many of the rhymes we know today have come from centuries back and have more than a grain of truth in them.

from The May Queen

You must wake and call me early, call me early,
    mother dear;
Tomorrow 'ill be the happiest time of all the glad
    New-year;
Of all the glad New-year, mother, the maddest
    merriest day,
For I'm to be Queen o' the May, mother, I'm to be
    Queen o' the May.

Alfred, Lord Tennyson
1809–92, b. England

Tennyson was a popular poet in his day. His work was admired by Prince Albert and this helped him become the national poet. Many of Tennyson's poems are on English history themes.

November

No sun – no moon!

No morn – no noon!

No dawn – no dusk – no proper time of day –

No sky – no earthly view –

No distance looking blue –

No road – no street – no 't'other side this way' –

No end to any Row –

No indications where the Crescents go –

No top to any steeple –

No recognitions of familiar people –

No courtesies for showing 'em –

No knowing 'em!

No travelling at all – no locomotion –

No inkling of the way – no notion –

'No go' by land or ocean –

No mail – no post –

No news from any foreign coast –

No Park, no Ring, no afternoon gentility –

No company – no nobility –

No warmth, no cheerfulness, no healthful ease,

No comfortable feel in any member –

No shade, no shine, no butterflies, no bees,

No fruits, no flowers, no leaves, no birds –

November!

Thomas Hood
1789–1845, b. England

Thomas Hood was both a writer and journalist and worked on a number of journals. He was highly regarded by other literary figures of the day, including Charles Dickens, and is particularly remembered for his humorous prose and verse.

The Wind

So wayward is the wind tonight
'Twill send the planets tumbling down;
And all the waving trees are light
In gauzes wafted from the moon.

Faint streaky wisps of roaming cloud
Are swiftly from the mountains swirl'd;
The wind is like a floating shroud
Wound light above the shivering world.

I think I see a little star
Entangled in a knotty tree,
As trembling fishes captured are
In nets from the eternal sea.

There seems a bevy in the air
Of spirits from the sparkling skies:
There seems a maiden with her hair
All tumbled in my blinded eyes.

O, how they whisper, how conspire,

And shrill to one another call!

I fear that, if they cannot tire,

The moon, her shining self, will fall.

Blow! Scatter even if you will

Like spray the stars about mine eyes!

Wind, overturn the goblet, spill

On me the everlasting skies!

Harold Munro

1879–1932, b. England

*H*arold Munro was the founder of the Poetry Bookshop in London in 1912. Wilfred Owen was said to have visited there many times. Munro wrote various anthologies of Georgian poetry and was a poet in his own right. When his Collected Works appeared posthumously in 1933, the introduction was written by his friend T S Eliot.

The Rainbow

My heart leaps up when I behold

A Rainbow in the sky:

So was it when my life began;

So is it now I am a man;

So be it when I shall grow old,

Or let me die!

The Child is father of the man;

And I could wish my days to be

Bound each to each by natural piety.

William Wordsworth
1770–1856, b. England

William Wordsworth's obvious joy in the English countryside is apparent in his poem 'The Rainbow' and is a theme in much of his poetry. He wrote some 70,000 lines of verse and is still a great favourite today.

Whether the Weather

Whether the weather be fine,

Or whether the weather be not,

Whether the weather be cold,

Or whether the weather be hot,

We'll weather the weather

Whatever the weather,

Whether we like it or not!

Author unknown

Sometimes it is said that the English language is difficult to learn and this verse with its same-sounding words or homonyms proves the point. This clever verse is a tongue-twister and its date and author are unknown.

from The Sun Rising

Busy old fool, unruly Sun,

Why dost thou thus,

Through windows, and through curtains, call on us?

Must to thy motions lovers' seasons run?

Saucy pedantic wretch, go chide

Late schoolboys, and sour prentices,

Go tell court-huntsmen that the king will ride,

Call country ants to harvest offices,

Love, all alike, no season knows, nor clime,

Nor hours, days, months, which are the rags of time.

Thy beams, so reverend and strong

Why shouldst thou think?

I could eclipse and cloud them with a wink,

But that I would not lose her sight so long:

If her eyes have not blinded thine,

Look, and tomorrow late, tell me

Whether both the Indias of spice and mine

Be where thou leftst them, or lie here with me.

Ask for those kings whom thou saw'st yesterday,

And thou shalt hear: 'All here in one bed lay.'

She's all states, and all princes I,

Nothing else is.

Princes do but play us; compar'd to this,

All honour's mimic, all wealth alchemy.

Thou, sun, art half as happy'as we,

In that the world's contracted thus;

Thine age asks ease, and since thy duties be

To warm the world, that's done in warming us.

Shine here to us, and thou art everywhere;

This bed thy centre is, these walls, thy sphere.

John Donne

1572–1631, b. England

The 16th-century poet and Churchman, John Donne, had an extensive knowledge of law, of the state and the Church, medicine and the classics. His work reflects this. He was one of the most important poets of his day though most of his famous work was published after his death.

from I Hear Thunder

(to the tune of 'Frère Jacques')

I hear thunder, I hear thunder,

Hark, don't you? Hark, don't you?

Pitter patter raindrops, pitter patter raindrops,

I'm wet through.

So are you.

Traditional rhyme

The verse *'I Hear Thunder' is a popular nursery rhyme loved by small children. The sing-song quality of the rhyme makes it easy to remember* *and the scary noises of thunder easily forgotten. The rhyme has been familiar for generations.*

Autumn Fires

In the other gardens
  And all up the vale,
From the autumn bonfires
  See the smoke trail!

Pleasant summer over
  And all the summer flowers,
The red fire blazes,
  The grey smoke towers.

Sing a song of seasons!
  Something bright in all!
Flowers in the summer,
  Fires in the fall!

Robert Louis Stevenson
1850–94, b. Scotland

*T*his poem by Robert Louis Stevenson has a fast moving rhythm and a childlike quality. It is easy to see the smoke rising from the bonfires, the orange flames of the fire and feel the autumnal air. It is from the collection **A Child's Garden of Verses,** *which first appeared in 1885.*

Bitter for Sweet

Summer is gone with all its roses,

Its sun and perfumes and sweet flowers,

Its warm air and refreshing showers:

And even Autumn closes.

Yea, Autumn's chilly self is going,

And winter comes which is yet colder;

Each day the hoar-frost waxes bolder,

And the last buds cease blowing.

Christina Rossetti
1830–94, b. England

Christina Rossetti is now considered to be one of the great Victorian poets. Few women from her time are acknowledged in the same way. Her poem 'Bitter for Sweet' heralds the onset of winter and she remembers the warmth of summer days and the chills of autumn.

The Twelve Months

Snowy, Flowy, Blowy,

Showery, Flowery, Bowery,

Hoppy, Croppy, Droppy,

Breezy, Sneezy, Freezy.

George Ellis
1753–1815, b. England

George Ellis was, according to his friend Sir Walter Scott, a great conversationalist. Ellis was a literary critic and satirist, and published volumes of selections of early poetical literature. His little verse 'The Twelve Months' is a brilliant summary of the whole year's weather.

A Rainy Day in April

When the clouds shake their hyssops, and the rain

Like holy water falls upon the plain,

'Tis sweet to gaze upon the springing grain

And see your harvest born.

And sweet the little breeze of melody

The blackbird puffs upon the budding tree,

While the wild poppy lights upon the lea

And blazes 'mid the corn.

The skylark soars the freshening shower to hail,

And the meek daisy holds aloft her pail.

And Spring all radiant by the wayside pale

Sets up her rock and reel.

See how she weaves her mantle fold on fold,

Hemming the woods and carpeting the wold.

Her warp is of the green, her woof the gold,

The spinning world her wheel.

Francis Ledwidge
1891–1917, b. Ireland

Francis Ledwidge left school aged 12 and worked on a farm, then on the roads and in the mines. Before entering World War I in 1914 he had already published verses in the Drogheda Times. *In 1915 he published* Songs of the Field, *having fought in Gallipoli, Salonika and Vardar. In 1916* Songs of Peace *was published. Francis Ledwidge fought at the Somme in France. He was killed at Boesinghe in Belgium in July 1917 by an exploding shell.*

Spring

Nothing is so beautiful as spring –

When weeds, in wheels, shoot long and lovely and lush;

Thrush's eggs look little low heavens, and thrush

Through the echoing timber does so rinse and wring

The ear, it strikes like lightnings to hear him sing;

The glassy peartree leaves and blooms, they brush

The descending blue; that blue is all in a rush

With richness; the racing lambs too have fair their fling.

What is all this juice and all this joy?

A strain of the earth's sweet being in the beginning

In Eden garden. – Have, get, before it cloy,

Before it cloud, Christ, lord, and sour with sinning,

Innocent mind and Mayday in girl and boy,

Most, O maid's child, thy choice and worthy the winning.

Gerard Manley Hopkins
1844–89, b. England

Gerard Manley Hopkins was raised in Hampstead in North London in the 1850s. The boy who went on to be a priest celebrated God's work in his poems and his great love of nature is evident in the poem 'Spring'.

Who Has Seen the Wind?

Who has seen the wind?

Neither I nor you:

But when the leaves hang trembling,

The wind is passing through.

Who has seen the wind?

Neither you nor I:

But when the trees bow down their heads,

The wind is passing by.

Christina Rossetti

1830–94, b. England

For a while Christina Rossetti helped her mother run a school in Somerset and though a lover of nature and happy to be in the countryside, she did not enjoy that time in her life. Despite her unhappy circumstances she produced some lovely observations of nature as seen in the two poems 'Who Has Seen the Wind?' and 'White Sheep'.

White Sheep

White sheep, white sheep on a blue hill.

When the wind stops, you all stand still.

When the wind blows, you walk away slow.

White sheep, white sheep, where do you go?

Christina Rossetti
1830–94, b. England

It's Raining, It's Pouring

It's raining, it's pouring,

The old man is snoring,

He went to bed and bumped his head,

And couldn't get up in the morning.

Traditional rhyme

Often nursery rhymes are learned long before a child can read. The nonsense nursery rhyme 'It's Raining, It's Pouring' is a great favourite with young children. This rhyme has passed down through the generations and its author is unknown.

Rain

The rain is falling all around,
It falls on field and tree,
It rains on the umbrellas here,
And on the ships at sea.

Robert Louis Stevenson

1850–94, b. Scotland

*T*his simple poem was included in Robert Louis Stevenson's A Child's Garden of Verses. Often confined to his bed due to illness as a child, it is easy to imagine Stevenson peering out of the window watching the world outside.

Blow, Blow, Thou Winter Wind

Blow, blow, thou winter wind,

Thou art not so unkind

As man's ingratitude;

Thy tooth is not so keen,

Because thou art not seen,

Although thy breath be rude.

Heigh-ho, sing heigh-ho! Unto the

green holly,

Most friendship is feigning, most loving mere folly.

Then heigh-ho the holly!

This life is most jolly.

Freeze, freeze, thou bitter sky,

That dost not bite so nigh

As benefits forgot;

Though thou the waters warp,

Thy sting is not so sharp

As friend rememb'red not.

Heigh-ho, sing heigh-ho! Unto the green holly,

Most friendship is feigning, most loving mere folly.

Then heigh-ho the holly!

This life is most jolly.

William Shakespeare

1564–1616, b. England

This song comes from William Shakespeare's comedy As You Like It. *He is probably the world's best-known playwright and is credited with having written 37 plays and 154 sonnets. Phrases like 'one fell swoop' and 'to the manner born' have percolated through from Shakespeare's work into common use today.*

Incy, Wincy Spider

Incy, Wincy spider
Climbed up the water spout;
Down came the rain
And washed the spider out:
Out came the sun
And dried up all the rain;
So Incy, Wincy spider
Climbed up the spout again.

Traditional rhyme

The verse about Incy, Wincy Spider is a counting and finger-moving game for young children and is ages old. Its origin is unknown.

Red Sky at Night

Red sky at night,

Shepherd's delight;

Red sky in the morning,

Shepherd's warning.

Traditional rhyme

The old verse 'Red Sky at Night' dates back in time. There is some form of it mentioned in the Bible (Matthew: 16).

It is not a totally reliable predictor of what the weather will do but there is some scientific basis to it.

LIFE AND DEATH

⸙

Whether the beginning of human life and
the death of innocence as portrayed in Milton's
Paradise Lost, or the transitory nature of life
and the quickness of death described in
'Sic Vita', or the down-to-earthly pleasures
of life in 'The Rubaiyat of Omar Khyayyam',
or Shakespeare's seven ages of man from
As You Like It, the following poems depict in
their different ways the same overriding truth:
life is short and death comes all too soon.

from Paradise Lost

In either hand the hastening angel caught

Our lingering parents, and to the eastern gate

Led them direct, and down the cliff as fast

To the subjected plain; then disappeared.

They looking back, all the eastern side beheld

Of Paradise, so late their happy seat,

Waved over by that flaming brand, the gate

With dreadful faces thronged and fiery arms;

Some natural tears they dropped, but wiped them soon;

The world was all before them, where to choose

Their place of rest, and providence their guide:

They hand in hand with wandering steps and slow,

Through Eden took their solitary way.

John Milton
1608–74, b. England

Paradise Lost *is John Milton's 12-book epic completed when he was entirely blind. First printed in 1667, it tells of the falls of Satan and subsequently, Man. Controversy exists over whether it champions free will above obedience to God. Milton rendered Satan so fascinating that some feel he emerges as the hero. In this, the closing extract, Adam and Eve wipe their tears perhaps suspiciously 'soon' as they are expelled from Eden. Some lines also suggest exciting possibilities rather than the misery of divine punishment.*

Sic Vita

Like to the falling of a star,
Or as the flights of eagles are,
Or like the fresh spring's gaudy hue,
Or silver drops of morning dew,
Or like a wind that chafes the flood,
Or bubbles which on water stood:
Even such is man, whose borrowed light
Is straight called in, and paid tonight.

   The wind blows out, the bubble dies;
   The spring entombed in autumn lies;
   The dew dries up, the star is shot;
   The flight is past: and man forgot.

Henry King
1592–1669, b. England

A friend of John Donne, Henry King began writing poetry while at Oxford University and later became Bishop of Chichester. Like 'Sic Vita', most of his poems involve either death itself or those who have died.

An unauthorized volume of his poems first appeared in 1657, the most famous being 'An Exequy to his Matchless never to be forgotten Friend' – a wonderful love poem on the passing of his wife.

461

from The Rubaiyat of Omar Khayyam

A Book of Verses

   underneath the Bough,

A Jug of Wine, a Loaf of

   Bread – and Thou

Beside me singing in

   the Wilderness –

O, Wilderness were

   Paradise enow!

Some for the Glories of This

   World; and some

Sigh for the Prophet's Paradise to come;

Ah, take the Cash, and let the Credit go,

Nor heed the rumble of a distant Drum!

Look to the blowing Rose about us – 'Lo,

Laughing,' she says, 'into the world I blow.

At once the silken tassel of my Purse

Tear, and its Treasure on the Garden throw.'

And those who husbanded the Golden grain

And those who flung it to the winds like Rain,

Alike to no such aureate Earth are turned

As, buried once, Men want dug up again.

The Worldly Hope men set their Hearts upon

Turns Ashes – or it prospers; and anon,

Like Snow upon the Desert's dusty Face,

Lighting a little hour or two – is gone.

Edward Fitzgerald
1809–83, b. England

Edward Fitzgerald's first book appeared at the age of 40 – a biography of the Quaker poet, Bernard Barton, whose daughter he later married. His other published works were largely translations, by far the most famous being his translations of the rubais or quatrains of the 12th-century Persian poet, Omar Khayyam. Fitzgerald's many letters to his friends Thackeray, Alfred and Frederick Tennyson, and Carlyle, are fascinating.

Remember

Remember me when I am gone away,

    Gone far away into the silent land;

    When you can no more hold me by the hand.

Nor I half turn to go yet turning stay.

Remember me when no more day by day

    You tell me of our future that you plann'd:

    Only remember me; you understand

It will be late to counsel then or pray.

Yet if you should forget me for a while

    And afterwards remember, do not grieve:

    For if the darkness and corruption leave

    A vestige of the thoughts that once I had,

Better by far you should forget and smile

    Than that you should remember and be sad.

Christina Rossetti
1830–94, b. England

*C*hristina Rossetti, like her mother and sister, was a devout High Anglican. As her life became severely restricted through continual ill health and caring for invalid relatives, she turned increasingly to her religious faith for strength and courage. In Poetical Works (published posthumously in 1904), her brother William, the editor, wrote: 'Death, as the avenue to a higher life, was contemplated by Christina Rossetti without nervousness or repulsion, even for the most part with desire…'

'Death Be Not Proud'

Death, be not proud, though some have callèd thee

    Mighty and dreadful, for thou art not so;

    For those whom thou think'st thou dost overthrow

Die not, poor Death, nor yet canst thou kill me.

From rest and sleep, which but thy pictures be,

    Much pleasure – then, from thee much more must flow;

    And soonest our best men with thee do go,

Rest of their bones and soul's delivery.

Thou'rt slave to fate, chance, kings and desperate men,

   And dost with poison, war, and sickness dwell;

   And poppy or charms can make us sleep as well,

And better than thy stroke. Why swell'st thou then?

   One short sleep past, we wake eternally,

   And death shall be no more. Death, thou shalt die.

John Donne
1572–1631, b. England

*J*ohn Donne's family were devout Catholics, although he grew to renounce his faith and as a Protestant became Dean of St Paul's (1621) – Donne's famous sermons are as fascinating as his poems. He is regarded as the founder of Metaphysical poetry – a style which explores paradox, novelty and ingenious comparisons, and often gives the effect of a speaking voice. This particular poem is one of the 'Holy Sonnets' Donne wrote, probably in 1610–11.

Because I Could not Stop for Death

Because I could not stop for Death –
   He kindly stopped for me –
   The Carriage held but just Ourselves –
   And Immortality.

We slowly drove – He knew no haste
   And I had put away
   My labour and my leisure too,
   For His Civility –

We passed the School, where Children strove
   At Recess – in the Ring –
   We passed the Fields of Gazing Grain –
   We passed the Setting Sun –

Or rather – He passed Us –
   The Dews drew quivering and chill –
   For only Gossamer, my Gown –
   My Tippet – only Tulle –

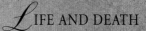

We paused before a House that seemed

   A Swelling of the Ground –

   The Roof was scarcely visible –

   The Cornice – in the Ground –

Since then – 'tis Centuries – and yet

   Feels shorter than the Day

   I first surmised the Horses' Heads

   Were toward Eternity –

Emily Dickinson
1830–86, b. USA

*A*lthough Emily Dickinson once actively sought publication for her poems, only seven poems were published during her lifetime. She seems to have accepted that she would remain unknown as a writer, yet over the years, her work became increasingly focused on herself as a poet, a mystic love for God, a playing on the value of life, and a fascination with death and immortality.

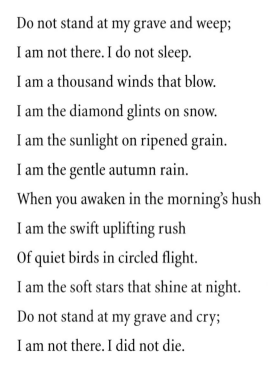

Do Not Stand At My Grave and Weep

Do not stand at my grave and weep;

I am not there. I do not sleep.

I am a thousand winds that blow.

I am the diamond glints on snow.

I am the sunlight on ripened grain.

I am the gentle autumn rain.

When you awaken in the morning's hush

I am the swift uplifting rush

Of quiet birds in circled flight.

I am the soft stars that shine at night.

Do not stand at my grave and cry;

I am not there. I did not die.

Anonymous

*S*oldier Steven Cummins was killed on active service in Northern Ireland. He left this anonymous poem in an envelope for his parents, to be opened in the event of his death. At first it was thought that Steven himself wrote it, but this was not the case. And although there have been other suggestions, such as 19th-century magazines and the prayers of Native American priests, the origins of the poem remain a mystery.

All the World's a Stage

All the world's a stage,

And all the men and women merely players;

They have their exits and their entrances,

And one man in his time plays many parts,

His acts being seven ages. At first the infant,

Mewling and puking in the nurse's arms.

Then the whining schoolboy, with his satchel

And shining morning face, creeping like snail

Unwillingly to school. And then the lover,

Sighing like furnace, with a woeful ballad

Made to his mistress' eyebrow. Then a soldier,

Full of strange oaths, and bearded like the pard,

Jealous in honour, sudden, and quick in quarrel,

Seeking the bubble reputation

Even in the cannon's mouth. And then the justice,

In fair round belly with good capon lin'd,

With eyes severe and beard of formal cut,

Full of wise saws and modern instances;

And so he plays his part. The sixth age shifts

Into the lean and slipper'd pantaloon,

With spectacles on nose, and pouch on side,

His youthful hose, well sav'd, a world too wide

For his shrunk shank, and his big manly voice,

Turning again toward childish treble, pipes

And whistles in his sound. Last scene of all,

That ends this strange eventful history,

Is second childishness, and mere oblivion,

Sans teeth, sans eyes, sans taste, sans every thing.

An extract from As You Like It
William Shakespeare
1564–1616, b. England

*S*hakespeare's plays often toy with the idea of the play itself. In the extract from As You Like It, *the melancholy speaker, Jacques, sees humans as predictable, forgettable actors performing a long meaningless farce. However, Shakespeare usually endows* both acting and life with the highest value. For instance, Hamlet watches a play to expose the truth about his father's murder. And several plays contain honourable female characters who dress up and act as men in order to set the world to rights.

from Ariel's Song

Full fathom five thy father lies,

    Of his bones are coral made;

Those are pearls that were his eyes,

    Nothing of him that doth fade,

But doth suffer a sea-change

Into something rich, and strange:

Sea-nymphs hourly ring his knell –

    Hark! now I hear them,

    Ding-dong bell.

William Shakespeare
1564–1616, b. England

Shakespeare's play The Tempest *is full of poetry and songs. It takes place on an island in faraway seas, the home of a strange band of characters: a magician called Prospero, his daughter Miranda, a spirit called Ariel who sings the song, and a sad monster called Caliban. Shakespeare was alive at a time when explorers, such as Francis Drake, were being sent on dangerous voyages, returning home with fantastic stories of strange animals and odd-looking people.*

Requiem

Under the wide and starry sky,

Dig the grave and let me lie,

Glad did I live and gladly die,

And I laid me down with a will.

This be the verse you grave for me:

Here he lies where he longed to be,

Home is the sailor, home from sea,

And the hunter home from the hill.

Robert Louis Stevenson
1850–94, b. Scotland

*T*he touching poem 'Requiem' written by Robert Louis Stevenson is made more poignant when one learns that the last two lines appear on his grave and that he selected them himself.

They Are Not Long

They are not long, the weeping and the laughter,

Love and desire and hate:

I think they have no portion in us after

We pass the gate.

They are not long, the days of wine and roses:

Out of a misty dream

Our path emerges for a while, then closes

Within a dream.

Ernest Dowson

1867–1900, b. England

Ernest Dowson left Oxford University without getting his degree and went to London to join a literary circle including Aubrey Beardsley and Oscar Wilde. He contributed to the infamous Yellow Book. Dowson also belonged to the Rhymers' Club which counted W B Yeats as a member. In 1891, Dowson converted to Roman Catholicism and this is reflected in some of his poetry. He travelled around London, France and Ireland after the death of his parents and wrote books of poetry, a play and translated the works of Voltaire, Zola and Balzac.

Young and Old

When all the world is young, lad,

And all the trees are green;

And every goose a swan, lad,

And every lass a queen;

Then hey for boot and horse, lad,

And round the world away!

Young blood must have its course, lad,

And every dog his day.

When all the world is old, lad,

And all the trees are brown;

And all the sport is stale, lad,

And all the wheels run down;

Creep home, and take your place there,

The spent and maimed among;

God grant you find one face there,

You loved when all was young.

Charles Kingsley
1819–75, b. England

*C*harles Kingsley was a man with many interests. He was a teacher, parson, editor and writer. In his best-remembered work The Water Babies he tackled many of the pressing issues of the time. He dealt with public health, pollution and the working conditions of the poor.

The Patriot

It was roses, roses, all the way,

With myrtle mixed in my path like mad.

The house-roofs seemed to heave and sway,

The church-spires flamed, such flags they had,

A year ago on this very day!

The air broke into a mist with bells,

The old walls rocked with the crowds and cries.

Had I said, 'Good folks, mere noise repels –

But give me your sun from yonder skies!'

They had answered, 'And afterward, what else?'

Alack, it was I who leaped at the sun,

To give it my loving friends to keep.

Nought man could do have I left undone,

And you see my harvest, what I reap

This very day, now a year is run.

There's nobody on the house-tops now –

Just a palsied few at the windows set –

For the best of the sight is, all allow,

At the Shambles' Gate – or, better yet,

By the very scaffold's foot, I trow.

I go in the rain, and, more than needs,

A rope cuts both my wrists behind,

And I think, by the feel, my forehead bleeds,

For they fling, whoever has a mind,

Stones at me for my year's misdeeds.

Thus I entered Brescia, and thus I go!

In such triumphs, people have dropped down dead.

'Thou, paid by the World, – what dost thou owe Me?'

God might have questioned; but now instead

'Tis God shall requite! I am safer so.

Robert Browning
1812–89, b. England

Robert Browning wanted to be a poet from his earliest days. He produced more poetry than almost any other English poet but was not appreciated by the public until he was well into his 50s. 'The Patriot' is a fine example of his dramatic style.

Life

Life, believe, is not a dream,

So dark as sages say;

Oft a little morning rain

Foretells a pleasant day:

Sometimes there are clouds of gloom,

But these are transient all;

If the shower will make the roses bloom,

Oh, why lament its fall?

   Rapidly, merrily,

Life's sunny hours flit by,

   Gratefully, cheerily,

Enjoy them as they fly.

What though death at times steps in,

And calls our Best away?

What though Sorrow seems to win,

O'er hope a heavy sway?

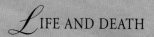

Yet Hope again elastic springs,

Unconquered, though she fell,

Still buoyant are her golden wings,

Still strong to bear us well.

   Manfully, fearlessly,

The day of trial bear,

   For gloriously, victoriously,

Can courage quell dispair!

Charlotte Brontë
1816–55, b. England

Charlotte Brontë was one of the three famous sisters who were all writing novels and poems at their home in Haworth on the Yorkshire moors in the early 1800s. They all led short, rather tragic lives. Charlotte is best known for her novels Jane Eyre (1847), Shirley (1848) and Villette (1853). Jane Eyre is still hugely popular today and was dedicated to the author William Makepeace Thackeray when first published.

LASTING CLASSICS

Some poems have become enduring by virtue of their simple language and timeless sentiments. William Blake's 'The Tyger' has become an evergreen, though written over 200 years ago, through its memorable cadences and intriguing imagery. Edgar Allen Poe's 'The Raven', with its haunting and troubling repetition of 'Nevermore' is a poem that, read once, will take up permanent residence in your memory. And Andrew Marvell's 'To His Coy Mistress', is a love poem with deep and sensual resonances that seem as fresh and meaningful today as they were when first written over three centuries ago.

The Tyger

Tyger! Tyger! burning bright
In the forests of the night,
What immortal hand or eye
Could frame thy fearful symmetry?

In what distant deeps or skies
Burnt the fire of thine eyes?
On what wings dare he aspire?
What the hand dare seize the fire?

And what shoulder, & what art,
Could twist the sinews of thy heart?
And when thy heart began to beat,
What dread hand? & what dread feet?

What the hammer? what the chain?
In what furnace was thy brain?
What the anvil? what dread grasp
Dare its deadly terrors clasp?

When the stars threw down their spears,

And water'd heaven with their tears,

Did he smile his work to see?

Did he who made the Lamb make thee?

Tyger! Tyger! burning bright

In the forests of the night,

What immortal hand or eye,

Dare frame thy fearful symmetry?

William Blake
1757–1827, b. England

William Blake worked as an engraver all his life and strove to be thought of as an artist rather than a poet. His first collection of poems was published in 1784, and the second – Songs of Innocence (1789) – he wrote, illustrated, engraved, printed, and sold himself. Blake was an independent thinker who rebelled against authority and developed a highly unorthodox, visionary interpretation of Christianity. 'The Tyger' appeared in Songs of Experience (1794).

from The Raven

Once upon a midnight dreary, while I pondered, weak and weary,
Over many a quaint and curious volume of forgotten lore –
While I nodded, nearly napping, suddenly there came a tapping,
As of someone gently rapping – rapping at my chamber door
''Tis some visitor,' I muttered, 'tapping at my chamber door –
    Only this and nothing more.'

Ah, distinctly I remember, it was in the bleak December,
And each separate dying ember wrought its ghost upon
    the floor.
Eagerly I wished the morrow; – vainly I had sought to borrow
From my books surcease of sorrow – sorrow for the lost Lenore –
For the rare and radiant maiden whom the angels name Lenore –
    Nameless here for evermore.
And the silken sad uncertain rustling of each purple curtain
Thrilled me – filled me with fantastic terrors never felt before:
So that now, to still the beating of my heart, I stood repeating
''Tis some visitor entreating entrance at my chamber door –
Some late visitor entreating entrance at my chamber door; –
    This it is and nothing more.'

Deep into that darkness peering, long I stood there wondering,
    fearing,
Doubting, dreaming dreams no mortal ever dared to dream before;
But the silence was unbroken, and the darkness gave no token,

And the only word there spoken was the whispered word, 'Lenore!' –
This I whispered, and an echo murmured back the word, 'Lenore!'
    Merely this and nothing more.
Then into the chamber turning, all my soul within me burning.

Soon again I heard a tapping somewhat louder than before.

'Surely,' said I, 'surely that is something at my window lattice;

Let me see, then, what thereat is, and this mystery explore –

Let my heart be still a moment, and this mystery explore; –

'Tis the wind and nothing more.'

Open here I flung the shutter, when, with many a flirt and flutter,

In there stepped a stately Raven of the saintly days of yore.

Not the least obeisance made he; not an instant stopped or stayed he;

But, with mien of lord or lady, perched above my chamber door –

Perched upon a bust of Pallas just above my chamber door –

    Perched, and sat, and nothing more.

Then this ebony bird beguiling my sad fancy into smiling,

By the grave and stern decorum of the countenance it wore,

'Though thy crest be shorn and shaven, thou,' I said, 'art sure no

    craven,

Ghastly grim and ancient Raven wandering from the Nightly shore –

Tell me what thy Lordly name is on the Night's Plutonian shore!'

    Quoth the Raven, 'Nevermore.'

But the Raven, sitting lonely on that placid bust, spoke only

That one word, as if his soul in that one word he did outpour.

Nothing further then he uttered; not a feather then he fluttered –

Till I scarcely more than muttered, 'Other friends have flown before –

On the morrow he will leave me, as my Hopes have flown before.'

    Then the bird said, 'Nevermore.'

'Prophet!' said I, 'thing of evil – prophet still, if bird or devil!

By that Heaven that bends above us – by that God we both adore –

Tell this soul with sorrow laden if, within the distant Aidenn,

It shall clasp a sainted maiden whom the angels name Lenore –

Clasp a rare and radiant maiden whom the angels name Lenore.'

Quoth the Raven, 'Nevermore.'

'Be that word our sign of parting, bird or fiend!' I shrieked,
   upstarting –

'Get thee back into the tempest and the Night's Plutonian shore!

Leave no black plume as a token of that lie thy soul hath spoken!

Leave my loneliness unbroken! – quit the bust above my door!'

Take thy beak from out my heart, and take thy form from off my
    door!'

    Quoth the Raven, 'Nevermore.'

And the Raven, never flitting, still is sitting – still is sitting

On the pallid bust of Pallas just above my chamber door;

And his eyes have all the seeming of a Demon's that is dreaming,

And the lamp-light o'er him streaming throws his shadow on the
    floor;

And my soul from out that shadow that lies floating on the floor
    Shall be lifted – nevermore!

Edgar Allen Poe
1809–49, b. USA

**J**ournalist Edgar Allen Poe was a master of macabre mystery stories such as **The Pit and the Pendulum.** _However, he began his writing career as a poet, publishing his first volume of verse in 1827 anonymously and at his own expense. 'The Raven' first appeared in 1845 in a New York newspaper, and_ **The Raven and other Poems** _(1845) finally brought him fame – although not fortune. He struggled with poverty, nervous instability and alcoholism and died at the age of 40._

Things Men Have Made

Things men have made with wakened hands, and put
    soft life into
are awake through years with transferred touch, and
    go on glowing for long years.
And for this reason, some old things are lovely
warm still with the life of forgotten men who made
    them.

D H Lawrence
1885–1930, b. England

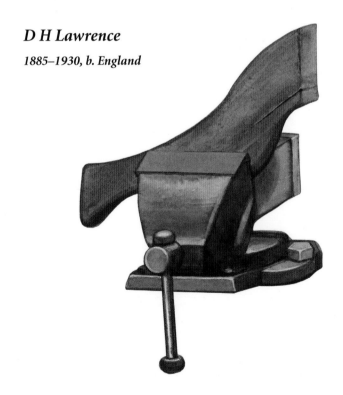

*D*avid Herbert Lawrence grew up in a mining village, experiencing the poverty and harshness of life after the Industrial Revolution. He came to loathe the dehumanizing factory processes and the crushing daily grind, believing that modern man was losing his ability to feel the quality of life. Lawrence is better known as a novelist than a poet, but both types of work share the honesty of feeling – both emotional and physical – that led to his works of fiction being labelled 'obscene'.

We Are
Fred Karno's Army

We are Fred Karno's army

The ragtime infantry

We cannot fight, we cannot shoot,

What earthly use are we!

And when we get to Berlin,

The Kaiser he will say,

'Hoch, hoch! Mein Gott,

What a bloody fine lot

Are the ragtime infantry!'

Anonymous

Fred Karno was the stage name of Frederick John Westcott who made and lost a fortune as a music-hall impresario. Karno developed a wonderful theatre and entertainment venue, The Karsino, on Tagg's Island on the River Thames, which was hugely successful until the end of World War I. Charlie Chaplin, Will Hay and Stan Laurel were among the talented troupe of comedians he employed.

To His Coy Mistress

Had we but world enough, and time,

This coyness Lady were no crime.

We would sit down and think which way

To walk, and pass our long love's day.

Thou by the Indian Ganges, side

Shouldst rubies find; I by the tide

Of Humber would complain. I would

Love you ten years before the flood,

And you should, if you please, refuse

Till the conversion of the Jews.

My vegetable love should grow

Vaster than empires and more slow;

An hundred years should go to praise

Thine eyes, and on thy forehead gaze;

Two hundred to adore each breast,

But thirty thousand to the rest;

An age at least to every part,

And the last age should show your heart.

For, lady, you deserve this state,

Nor would I love at lower rate.

But at my back I always hear

Times winged chariot hurrying near;

And yonder all before us lie

Deserts of vast eternity.

Thy beauty shall no more be found;

Nor, in thy marble vault shall sound

My echoing song; then worms shall try

That long preserved virginity,

And your quaint honor turn to dust,

And into ashes all my lust:

The grave's a fine and private place,

But none, I think, do there embrace.

Now therefore while the youthful hue

Sits on thy skin like morning dew,

And while thy willing soul transpires

At every pore with instant fires,

Now let us sport us while we may,

And now, like amorous birds of prey,

Rather at once our time devour

Than languish in his slow-chapped power.

Let us roll all our strength and all

Our sweetness up into one ball,

And tear our pleasures with rough strife

Thorough the iron gates of life:

Thus, though we cannot make our sun

Stand still, yet we will make him run.

Andrew Marvell
1621–78, b. England

The poem 'To His Coy Mistress' was written in the 17th century when England began to explore and discover exotic locations. In this poem Andrew Marvell conjures up the image of the River Ganges alongside his own home territory of the Humber in Yorkshire. Marvell composed lyric poetry, which was sensuous, elegant and sometimes passionate, and as a politician and poet often wrote about contemporary political questions.

La Belle Dame Sans Merci

Ah what can ail thee, wretched wight,
    Alone and palely loitering?
The sedge has wither'd from the lake,
    And no birds sing.

Ah what can ail thee, wretched wight,
    So haggard and so woe-begone?
The squirrel's granary is full,
    And the harvest's done.

I see a lilly on thy brow
    With anguish moist and fever dew,
And on thy cheeks a fading rose
    Fast withereth too.

I met a lady in the meads,
    Full beautiful, a faery's child;
Her hair was long, her foot was light,
    And her eyes were wild.

I set her on my pacing steed,
And nothing else saw all day long,
For sideways would she bend, and sing
A faery's song.

I made a garland for her head,
And bracelets too, and fragrant zone;
She look'd at me as she did love,
And made sweet moan.

She found me roots of relish sweet,
And honey wild, and manna dew,
And sure in language strange she said,
I love thee true.

She took me to her elfin grot,
And there she wept, and sigh'd deep,
And there I shut her wild sad eyes-
So kiss'd to sleep.

'And there we slumbered on the moss,
  And there I dream'd, ah woe betide,
The latest dream I ever dream'd
  On the cold hill side.

'I saw pale kings and princes too,
  Pale warriors, death-pale were they all;
Who cried – "La belle Dame sans Merci
  Hath thee in thrall!"

'I saw their starv'd lips in the gloam,
  With horrid warning gaped wide,
And I awoke and found me here,
  On the cold hill side.

'And this is why I sojourn here,
  Alone and palely loitering,
Though the sedge is wither'd from the lake,
  And no birds sing.'

John Keats
1795–1821, b. England

*J*ohn Keats wrote 'La Belle Dame Sans Merci' in April 1819. It is said that shortly before writing the poem he recorded a dream in which he met a beautiful woman in a magic place, which was full of pale, enslaved lovers. He had also been reading Spenser's The Faerie Queene in which an enchantress appears.

*I*NDEX OF FIRST LINES

# Acknowledgements

The publishers would like to thank the following new sources
who have contributed to this book:

Cover Beach Walk, 1994 by Easton, Timothy Bridgeman;
Page 73 Bettmann/CORBIS; 83 Jennifer Hunt; 199 Marilyn Barbone/Fotolia;
282 The Art Archive/Musee National d'art moderne Paris/Dagli Orti;
340 Jim Miles.

All other images are from:

Miles Kelly Artwork Bank, Corel, digitalSTOCK,
iStockphoto.com, PhotoDisc John Foxx, PhotoAlto